- NW

YOUR SEXUAL BILL OF RIGHTS

Your Sexual Bill of Rights

An Analysis of the Harmful Effects of Sexual Prohibitions

Leonard V. Ramer

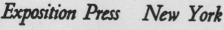
Exposition Press   New York

First Printing, 1975
Second Printing, 1975
Third Printing, 1976
Fourth Printing, 1976
Fifth Printing, 1977

EXPOSITION PRESS
900 South Oyster Bay Rd., Hicksville, N.Y. 11801

LIBRARY OF CONGRESS CATALOG CARD NUMBER: 72-94861

ISBN 0-682-48766-X

To my brother, Ernest Ramer,
Through whose efforts this book was published

Also to William A. Donohoe
and George Cohee

Contents

YOUR SEXUAL BILL OF RIGHTS

Introduction

Approximately twenty-five years ago I began a study of human sexuality because it seemed to me that the evils of sex were exaggerated out of all realistic proportions. I could not understand how a perfect God could create a function of the human body as evil as religion and the law made it out to be. My curiosity having been aroused, I began a search for the latest biological and psychological facts. With the words of Marcus Aurelius in mind—"For I search after truth, by which man was never yet been harmed. But he is harmed who abideth in his deception and ignorance"—I began collecting sexual information.

Realizing the importance of obtaining this information from reliable and recognized authorities of national and worldwide prominence, I obtained such books as Kinsey's *Sexual Behavior in the Human Male*, Reich's *The Function of the Orgasm*, Cole's *Sex and Love in the Bible*, Blanton's *Love or Perish*, Berg and Allan's *The Problem of Homosexuality*, Coleman's *Freedom From Fear*, Duffy's *Sex and Crime*, and Fishman's *Sex in Prison*, plus many more.

Gradually, through the years, I obtained a most amazing and shocking picture of human sexual ignorance. I found that the facts I thought were true were based on a combination of superstition, myths, and ignorance.

Most appalling of all was the inescapable conclusion that, in the United States especially, the most demoralizing social problem of them all was an unnatural and unrealistic negative attitude toward our sexual nature.

This attitude, I discovered, was creating incredible psychological damage in the form of irrational sexual shame, irrational sexual guilt, irrational sexual fears, and irrational self-hatred. Until a few years ago even the word "sex" was a dirty word; consequently, if you had the courage to as much as suggest that a social problem had sexual roots you would be ostracized by society. Even today, with the exception of many prescient authorities, most of us have no idea that the cause of such seemingly insoluble social problems as crime, suicide, divorce, juvenile delinquency, and alcoholism is to be found in sexual ignorance and maladjustment. We have no idea of the fantastically demoralizing effects of sexual shame, sexual guilt, and sexual fears, which generate a conscious or unconscious hatred of sex in all of us.

If you were to draw a picture of a giant octopus covering the United States, with its body representing sexual fears and each tentacle representing a different problem stemming from sexual fears —crime, murder, divorce, neurosis, psychosis, tension-caused diseases, suicide, blackmail, assaults, violence, alcoholism, drug addiction, compulsive gambling, sexual perversions, homosexuality, frigid woman, impotent men, abortion, juvenile delinquency, sexual gossip, and sexual hypocrisy—that picture might suggest to you the truly enormous magnitude of the damage inflicted by our unnatural sexual attitudes and their resulting sexual shame, guilt, and fears.

Even as recently as 1969, a newspaper article summarizing the origins and causes of violence in the United States never so much as mentioned our irrational sexual fears as a basic cause. Authorities, seeking to get to the rock bottom of much of our violence, are still fruitlessly attempting to treat the symptoms instead of curing the disease.

After reading case histories such as Lindner's *Rebel Without a Cause,* and Freeman's *Before I Kill More* and considering their sexual implications, I came to the conclusion that without a doubt a vast amount of human anxiety, frustration, suffering, torture, and agony come from the unnecessary and unnatural sexual conflicts stemming from our appalling sexual ignorance. We are, in fact, literally being crucified on the cross of sexual fears by an attitude of sexual bigotry instilled in us through false religious theories and antiquated and unenforceable penal laws that have never been changed to correspond with the biological and psychological truths of human sexuality. Reason and common sense tell anyone willing to learn the truth that ancient out-of-date religious beliefs must of necessity be replaced by the latest scientific discoveries. It is self-evident that the Bible cannot be used as a textbook in the psychology or biology of sex, and it cannot be substituted for the natural laws controlling the functioning of the nerves, glands, or muscles of the human body.

Because human beings naturally fear and thus automatically hate the unknown, it is my hope that, by a presentation of facts vital to the living of a natural sex life, I can help eliminate at least some of the unnatural and irrational shame, guilt, and fear of any reasonable, sensible, and harmless sexual activity.

Human beings are sexual beings, with sex the motivating force in their lives. Human sexuality is not an invention of the devil but the creation of God, bestowed on us for joy, happiness, and as the source of all love. Of all of the marvels of the human body, the most phenomenal and wonderful are the sex organs, which without question surpass any invention man has ever developed or ever will develop. Rejection of any biologically determined use of the sexual organs is nothing less than the rejection of the natural laws as determined by God. To call them wicked and dirty is a repudiation of God Himself and a denial of His right to create us as He desired us.

Because through circumstance I had developed the interest, the incentive, and the desire, and because I took the necessary time, I was able to dig out material that painted an amazing picture of a society chained to a sexual life of fear, self-hatred, suffering, torture and agony—a society plagued by innumerable social problems that it did not understand or realize were rooted in an ignorant and unnatural attitude toward a biological sexual nature that could not be altered or changed by laws or prohibitions. It was a society that acted as if sex were a necessary evil rather than a biological necessity and a source of human joy, happiness, and peace of mind; a society that does nothing to abolish an obsolete sexual penal code that has long since become a monstrous absurdity, unenforceable and unobserved by 95 percent of the population, but which, since it is still "the law" remains a source of underlying apprehension and guilt.

My sincere hope is that the information presented here will become available to the many individuals whose lives have been demoralized by harassing and destructive sexual guilt and fears. Knowledge and understanding of our true sexual nature cannot help but alleviate much of the agony and torture caused by unnatural and unrealistic sexual beliefs. Most individuals, whether they are conscious of it or not, cannot help having a more or less damaging mental conflict rage between their natural instincts and the antiquated religious and legal sexual prohibitions. No one should be driven into the violence and rebellion often caused by the dreadful and demoralizing self-hatred that frequently develops from fear and hatred of one's own unconquerable sexual nature. Every human being should be entitled to his natural sexual birthright, with the freedom to choose his own type of sexual activity, as long as it is nonviolent, noncoercive, satisfactory, private, and harmless to others. The inescapable truth is that our mental and physical health are absolutely dependent on living a happy sex life free from guilt and fear.

With a deep sense of compassion for all sexually tortured human beings—and that is most of us—I present the following facts in the spirit of the words of Etienne de Grollet:

> I shall pass through this world but once. Any good, therefore, that I can do or any kindness that I can show to any human being, let me do it now. Let me not defer it or neglect it for I shall not pass this way again.

The cycle of fear and hate and guilt play a continual role in the misconceptions characteristic of sex taboos. *Sex is associated with shame. Shame is the prelude to guilt, and guilt is the beginning of fear.* The terrible and dangerous age of sex (childhood) is an expendable bogeyman *that must be destroyed to insure adult happiness.*

DR. LESTER L. COLEMAN

A tragic and agonizing fear grips tens of millions of Americans, demoralizing and shattering their lives and destroying their peace of mind and happiness. Amazingly, the cause does not enter their minds. In fact most people would probably swear they had no fears of sex, and that sex had nothing to do with their troubles and afflictions. Nevertheless, hidden deep within their unconscious minds is a religiously and legally induced guilt over and fear of every sexual thought, word, and deed.

Fear is the *world's greatest problem. Fear* is the *world's greatest menace.* Fear is everywhere. It infiltrates our physical, mental, and spiritual beings, overwhelming and conquering us by its very force. It is a contagious disease, spreading and engulfing all those around us. It cripples and paralyzes. It distorts our personalities and behavior. It robs us of our happiness, tranquility, and peace of mind. It displays itself in the form of greed, selfishness, shyness, hostility, anger, aggressiveness, and hatred. It multiplies and is compounded until we function more like animals than human beings, or, possibly, are unable to function at all.

And that is not all. It plays havoc with careers, social attainments, relationships between man and wife, relationships between parents and children, relationships between friends, neighbors, and relatives, relationships between pastors and parishioners, and even the relationship between man and God. Pastors who use unnatural fear as a club with which to beat their parishioners into obedience, who stress fear of the wrath of God, who threaten them with God's terrible punishment are in effect attempting to frighten people into heaven. It is a psychological fact that you simply do not love what you fear—you hate it because you fear whatever seems to be a threat to your well-being or safety.

Dr. Lester L. Coleman, one of America's foremost physicians and an expert on the subject of fear, gives us a clear explanation of sexual fear in his book *Freedom From Fear.*

> Adult [sexual] problems have been traced *repeatedly to the initial source of shame, fear, and guilt.* It is born in childhood, allowed to expand during adolescence, and begins to show its affects in the adult.
>
> Some authorities say up to 40 percent of all divorces can be traced *to the man's or woman's refusal to participate in normal sexual relationships.* Often, the basis of refusal *is an impression gained in childhood that sexual activity is evil and should be punished. . . . [This fact should make pastors stop and think.]*
>
> Misconceptions born in the ignorance of sex education are not easily (if at all) eradicated in adult life. *Psychological distortions of the true meaning of sex learned haphazardly in adolescence are deep-rooted.* It is false *to assume that these misconceptions spontaneously eradicate themselves as people advance in years.* Fears in the adult are the heavy penalty for inadequate sex knowledge. . . . Experts variously estimate that emotional confusion and psychological instability are *responsible for almost 40 percent of infertile women.*
>
> These are the penalties the adult pays in fear and anxiety which have their roots in childhood. These are some of the penalties that a child *unnecessarily pays for having been deprived of its normal birthright to be shown that there is no shame in true knowledge of how the body and mind function. Fear and ignorance have no defense against understanding and knowledge.*

Most sex fears, therefore, are deadly destroyers of mental and physical health. They are unnatural, irrational, and unrealistic. They are at the roots of many of our most tragic social problems. They breed aggression, violence, and war. The evil is not in the sensible use of sex but in the tremendously destructive evils of *our false, unnatural, and ignorant attitudes toward sex. After all it is a creation of God.*

Many startling facts were recently disclosed by one of our great prison wardens, Clinton Duffy. He states that 90 percent of all criminals were in prison *because of sexual guilt, sexual fears, sexual frustration, and sexual ignorance.* Amazingly, 90 percent of *crime has its origin in sexual problems* of one kind or another. We should emphasize this: *The source of most crime is in sexual ignorance and fears.* From the moment sex becomes associated with shame we follow a disastrous path of psychological reactions.

First, shame, planted in the child by guilt-laden parents, grows into an unconscious guilt over all sexual thoughts and activity.

Second, sexual guilt automatically grows into sexual fears. Usually, we fear anything that is a threat to us in any form. Because sex *is not a danger to be combated, fear of sex is an unnatural, abnormal, and irrational fear.*

Third, because fear of anything causes us to hate the thing feared, fear of sex soon develops into hatred of all things sexual.

Fourth, hatred of our own sexuality, and of our own God-given bodies because of their sexual organs soon develops into a deadly and destructive *self-hatred —a self-hatred we do not understand and may even be unaware of,* a self-hatred that *often explodes into violence and aggression.*

One enormously damaging cause of self-hatred is the inevitable and destructive tug-of-war *between our natural sex instincts, which cannot be conquered, and our unnatural religious beliefs, which we vainly attempt to live up to, plus the threat of biologically and psychologically false sexual penal laws.*

Fifth, self-hatred breeds violence; it breeds aggression; it breeds brutality; it breeds rebellion; and it may even breed war. Self-hating parents develop self-hating children who often grow up to be criminals, alcoholics, drug addicts, murderers, suicides, and mental cases.

If we would invest sufficient funds in serious research probing to a sufficient depth—in other words, get down to the rock bottom —to discover the causes of many of our most aggravating and serious social problems, which are disastrously damaging and costly to society, we would find that a very large percentage of them have sexual maladjustment of various types as the basic cause. Although the public is beginning to understand that sex is a natural function determined by the natural laws, vast numbers of people know nothing of its effects on the living of a natural life and ignorantly seek to prevent any kind of sexual research because they believe sex is too evil to be discussed.

Even the public uproar of a small minority can and does discourage the finding of research on the sexuality of man. Although many authorities probably realize the catastrophic consequences of our false sexual attitudes, they are unwilling to expose themselves to the attacks of sexual fanatics who may even stigmatize them as sexual maniacs. Unfortunately, leaders who tenaciously cling to ancient sexual beliefs in spite of recent scientific discoveries, and pastors who seemingly are unable to use anything but the negative approach to sexuality, are responsible for much of the intolerance toward sex.

To the sexually superstitious and ignorant persons the following list of social problems rooted in false and unnatural sex attitudes may very well seem unbelievable. Even open-minded people may be amazed at the enormous amount of damage occurring from sexual shame, guilt, fears, frustrations, and tensions.

The following list of social plagues, staggering as it may be, nevertheless is rooted in sexual ignorance, false sexual beliefs, sexual superstitions, and irrational sexual fears and attitudes. Hidden unconscious sexual fears can too often block open recognition of the truth because of reluctance to lose face by an admission that long-accepted sexual beliefs are false. Only sensible sexual education can free us from the chains of sexual fears. Unquestionably, it is an obligation to God to use the intelligence and reasoning powers He endowed us with to lighten the awful burden of our irrational sexual fears.

We might begin the list with *crime, one of our most costly social problems,* which is estimated by some unimpeachable authorities to be 90 percent sexually based, thus making criminality a sexual problem.

Murder (probably 90 percent rooted in sexual frustrations and fears).

Violence and destructiveness (a large though unknown amount is caused by anger over sexual frustration and denial of sexual gratification).

Blackmail (almost totally a sexual problem because our impossible sexual laws by their very nature, provide the victims).

Suicide (a very large percentage of suicides are victims of sexual fears and frustrations too overwhelming to bear).

Alcoholism and drunkenness (recognized by many authorities to have sexual conflicts as a root cause.

Psychosis (mental disease, known as insanity, and often rooted in sexual guilt and fears.)

Neurosis (Reich found *all* neurotic patients had mental conflicts over the thwarting of their natural sexual urges).

Compulsive gambling (probably a sexual perversion).

Sexual perversions (caused by the unnatural blocking of the natural sexual urges by sexual fears).

Frigid women and impotent men (probably 85 percent result from guilt over and fear of sexual functioning).

Juvenile delinquency and unrest (probably the major causes are concealed sexual conflicts and sexual frustrations).

Homosexuality as a condition, not as an added sexual outlet (often caused by fears of the opposite sex induced in childhood by the sexual fears imparted by parents).

Pornography (an outlet for unsatisfied release of sexual tensions and unsatisfied sexual curiosity).

Sexual gossip (a major part of gossip is over illegal and condemned sexual activity, whether imagined or real).

Sexual hypocrisy (we condemn legally prohibited sexual activity in public and practice it in private, which makes us a nation of sexual hypocrites).

There is no question that the sexual penal laws and the sexual attitudes of many religious leaders, with their attempted blocking of the sex drive, have been the cause of enormous amounts of human agony. The lack of knowledge and understanding of human sexuality is plainly the most demoralizing of all human afflictions and is an appalling example of what happens when man attempts to block a natural urge. The above list should be sufficient proof.

Our attitudes about sex are indeed terrifying because of their sheer ignorance and stupidity. Many of us act *as if God himself* created our bodies to be something too dirty to be seen unclothed.

Nothing is more revolting than the *implications* one sees in the words and actions of some religious leaders and public figures that *God, the creator of sex, is a dirty, wicked, sinful, obscene, and immoral God. If God is a dirty, nasty God,* we might call the human body and its sexual function the same: however, because *He cannot be anything but the essence of wisdom and perfection, then sex logically and necessarily, has to be good and wholesome in His eyes because He created it.*

Man, and man himself, has twisted and distorted sex into a wicked and obscene activity by his false conceptions and his warped mental attitudes. Man himself, in his superstitions, and in his biological and psychological ignorance, has made sex into an evil that God himself *never intended.*

Ancient *biblical quotations* may have indicated the sexual knowledge and ideas of man two or three thousand years ago but unquestionably have been *replaced by the biological and psychological facts of today.* Religion and the state might as well recognize the realities of human sexuality because they cannot possibly fit the human body into the frame work of ancient superstitions and religious theories *in direct contradiction to the natural laws.*

Sex, in spite of beliefs to the contrary, is not a sacred function of the body (how in the name of common sense can we call sex "dirty" and "nasty" and then, in the next breath, call it "sacred"?) but an essential biological function. It is not a spiritual matter but a biological necessity for good mental and physical health, comparable to eating, drinking, and sleeping. It is not a matter of willpower or something imagined but a matter of release of sexual tensions and expelling sexual liquids when the sex glands are full. It is not a luxury but a necessity. It is no more a sin than the other essential functions of the body; like everything else, however, *it can be used for evil purposes.*

The so-called immorality of sex, in any harmless way, is a myth. The word "immoral" has become so overworked in connection with sex that it has almost become synonomous with sex. When we see it used in the newspapers, we immediately associate it with some forbidden sex act. This, of course, is absurd. *Any sin we commit is immoral,* whether it is blackmail, false advertising, gossip, or adultery. To label immoral anything your body compels you to do—in anything that obeys natural laws—is a gross misrepresentation.

Another absurdity in human sexuality is abstinence. We may glibly talk about sexual abstinence as a method to curb our sexual activity, but no one, if he is mentally and physically healthy, can escape the natural sexual demands of his body. If it is his misfortune to be a sexual cripple or to have a weak sex drive, he will have little if any compulsion for sexual activity. Abstinence from sexual activity then becomes no problem at all. Because nature demands constant exercise of the muscles and nerves for a healthy body, the absence of exercise of the sexual organs and nerves will eventually cause them to atrophy—shrink—until they become paralyzed and useless.

The inescapable truth is that *God did not design the human body for sexual abstinence.* When the sex glands of the male need draining *they must be drained,* just as the bladder must be drained. There is no possibility of turning sex on and off like a water faucet or an electric light, as numerous clergymen seem to believe. When sex glands are full it is as useless *to tell a male* to get his mind on something else as it would to tell a person with a full bladder to forget about it.

After the arrival of sexual maturity (at twelve to fourteen years) *nature has made expulsion of sexual liquids mandatory,* whether we like it or not.

Because youngsters of that age are not in the position to marry, masturbation, contrary to the opinions of many people, *should be encouraged,* certainly it should not be discouraged. It was discovered long ago that masturbation, instead of being the monster it was alleged to be, was natural, healthy, and perfectly harmless. Many people still have the idea that nocturnal or wet dreams provide a natural outlet; Kinsey, however, found that they provided a much smaller amount of relief than imagined, with 17 percent of males never having them.

The public, the legislators, the clergy, and even the medical profession give little evidence of having a true conception of the incredible amount of mental and physical illness caused by the terrible inroads of sexual fears. Neither do they realize the number of social disorders that have their origin in sexual shame, sexual fears, sexual tensions, sexual anxieties, and sexual frustrations.

Suffering, agony, and torture constitute the price we pay for acting as if God's most wonderful and delightful gifts to man were a dirty and obscene activity. Even the primitive peoples who did not know God respected sex to the extent that they worshipped it as the god of fertility and creation. How is it possible that we who know Him as a God of love, stupidly condemn His creation as evil, dirty, and nasty?

Ignorance of the biological and psychological truths of human sexuality may be an excuse, but it should not be tolerated in a supposedly God-fearing and civilized nation. As an ancient philosopher once said, *"Ignorance is the greatest crime of all—for it is a crime against the mind."*

Today's sin is the sin of ignorance where knowledge is available, of failing to seek for more knowledge now that we have the means of seeking it, or failing to believe that the truth will make us free.

MARGARET MEAD

An appalling number of our most serious social problems, if traced to their ultimate source, will be found rooted in either a conscious or unconscious fear of sex. Unfortunately, most people do not have the remotest idea that sexual conflicts have anything to do with these problems. Society goes on its merry way stupidly spending billions upon billions in vain and fruitless efforts *to treat the symptoms* but few make any effort *to treat the disease,* probably because they have never been taught the importance of human sexuality to their physical and mental health.

Human beings are born with six vital functions of the body. These functions are of supreme importance. They are the natural laws of God and *must be used properly* if full mental and physical health is to be achieved. All of us, if we stop a moment to think, will easily see that eating, drinking, breathing, sleeping, and eliminating bodily wastes are absolutely essential. What we do not seem to be aware of is that a sixth—releasing sexual tensions—is by natural law as necessary as the other five for a healthy and happy life.

Most of us understand and realize the physical damage we suffer if we eat too much or go without food; if we drink too much water or are forced to go without, if we do not get sufficient rest and sleep, or if we are unable to urinate or evacuate the bowels. *What we do not seem to know or understand is that if sexual tensions are not relieved and sexual liquids are not expelled (in the male) our mental and bodily health can be seriously damaged.*

Religion seems to pay little attention to other natural functions of the human body, but when it comes to sex, it has for centuries attempted by every device to frighten us away from its use as though it was invented by the devil himself. Religious beliefs, no matter how strong, *cannot prevent the manufacture of sexual fluids by the body.* Neither can religious beliefs *stop the human body from building up nervous sexual tensions. God Himself determined* the sexuality of man when He created him. Who are we to attempt to change the natural biological functioning of the human body with puny sex regulations and man-made laws?

All of us can recall incidents in our lives when our bladders became full—so full that urination became a dire necessity. Similarly, the sex glands in males become painfully full and ejaculation becomes imperative. It not only becomes painful at times, but the body is almost overwhelmed with nervous sexual tensions *that must be relieved.*

History shows us, through man's sexual conduct during the wars of the past, that it is impossible to block the sex drive. Large bodies of men, grouped together without access to women, either turned to homosexuality or indulged in mass rape. Men without an available sexual outlet are much like a group of people starving for lack of food. History has recorded times when the strong have turned on the weak and devoured them. To starving people, cannibalism was plainly a lesser evil than starvation.

Prison riots are easily understandable to anyone with knowledge of the power of the sex drive. Probably 95 percent of them could be prevented by the simple method of permitting or providing sexual outlets for sex-starved inmates. A society intent on revenge on the lawbreakers demands sexual starvation as a part of the punishment. The irony of the frequent exposure of homosexuality in prisons is the public *reaction* over such "terrible conditions." The public seems to have no idea *that they themselves are responsible for forcing these conditions on prisons.* All prisons, as they are now constituted, *can be nothing but hotbeds of homosexuality.* Prison authorities, if they are honest about the matter, recognize and admit that prison riots are caused almost exclusively *by men driven frantic by their sexual hunger* for the *purpose of engaging in homosexual orgies.*

Protesters against the natural laws of sex should invent detachable sex organs that could be separated from the prisoners' bodies as the convicted enter prison, stored away, and then be taken out of storage and returned when they are discharged. This could solve the problem—if it were possible. Unless society awakens and provides sexual freedom in the prisons, prison riots will continue at the cost of millions to the public.

Dr. Smily Blanton's excellent explanation of the *true meaning of sex* in *Love or Perish* states:

> Human beings are sexual beings and it is now generally accepted that *sex is a normal and necessary* [note the *necessary*] part of our lives. . . . *Men follow a futile goal* when they seek to obtain sublimity of love *through a total denial of its basic source.* Our true aspiration must be rather *to achieve control of our primitive nature* [note to *achieve control*—not *abstinence,* not *continence,* not *purity*] so we may employ our normal energies in the best interest of mankind. *To attempt the abandonment of the primitive heritage is more than impossible: it can only release the very demons we hope to exorcise.*

In *The Function of the Orgasm* Dr. Wilhelm Reich observes:

> *The natural instincts are biological facts which can neither be defaced from the earth nor be basically altered.* [Let me repeat: *neither be defaced from the earth nor basically altered.*] Like everything living man needs first of all satisfaction of his hunger and *gratification of his sexual instinct.*

The one supremely vital fact that society must recognize for its own welfare is that *we are created by an act of God to be sexual beings and we must put an end to feeling shame and guilt and fear over our sexuality. We must cease hating ourselves for our sexual nature. There can be no wickedness or evil in acting as God created us to act.*

Let's examine some of the devastating social problems we make for ourselves through our own sexual shame, guilt, and fear. Human scourges they are and human scourges they will remain until we have the common sense to overcome our hidden and repressed fears of sex.

1. Nervous tensions. Tensions have been found by scientific research to be the cause of many of the diseases tormenting humanity. There is no doubt that sexual tensions caused by sexual frustrations and sexual anxieties are one of the leading tensions. Harassed and tortured by sexual tensions, we become victims of neurosis or psychosis and numerous physical diseases.

Dr. Wilhelm Reich, one of the world's great psychologists, blames *improper and insufficient release* of sexual tensions as the *cause of all neurosis.* This does not at all seem impossible when we consider the deadly tug-of-war constantly waged between *man's natural sexual urges* and the *unnatural religious restrictions, plus the unnatural state sex laws.* The combination guarantees the creation of destructive sexual tensions.

2. Crime "Sex is the cause of nearly all crime, the dominant force that drives nearly all criminals." This quoted statement seems unbelievable and even fantastic to all those good people who believe that sex is a figment of the imagination and have no conception of the horrors of sexual shame, guilt, and fear.

It is the statement of no less than Clinton T. Duffy, former warden of San Quentin and one of the foremost penologists of the United States, in his book *Sex and Crime.* He estimates that 90 percent of the men in our prisons are there because of *sexual anxieties, sexual doubts, sexual tensions, or sexual problems* of one sort or another.

Dr. Albert Ellis, the New York psychotherapist, reported to the American Association for the Advancement of Science that countless instances of crime—such as many cases of arson, shootings, and burglary—that "appear," on the surface, to be devoid of any sexual element are *actually caused by the criminal's conscious or unconscious sexual urges and needs.* Indeed, it is possible that there is a strong, *although hidden, sex factor in the majority of nonsex crimes.*

Unfortunately, law enforcement officials, legislators, and others concerned with lawlessness appear oblivious to the supreme importance of sex maladjustment in the crime picture.

3. Violence and destructiveness. We search, we investigate, we study, and we guess at the causes of violence and destructiveness without ever considering sex in the form of sexual frustration, sexual anxiety, sexual tensions, and sexual fears as the root cause. Reich declares:

> The destructiveness which is bound up in the character *is nothing but the anger about frustration in general and denial of sexual gratification in particular.* If analysis *penetrated to a sufficient depth* every destructive tendency *gave way to a sexual one.* Destructive tendencies were shown to be nothing but reactions; reactions to disappointment in love or the loss of love. *If the desire for love or for satisfaction of the sex urge meets with insuperable obstacles, one begins to hate.*

Incredibly, in a newspaper article summarizing the origin and causes of American violence, Charles and Bonnie Remsberg (writers for the National Commission on the Causes and Prevention of Violence) *never even mentioned sexual maladjustment* as having any connection or as being the root cause of much of the violence. Whether they were unaware of it or the studies they mentioned had not penetrated to a sufficient depth is unknown. Or could it be that sex is considered such an evil that most authorities unconsciously evade the study of its effects on humanity?

Dr. Albert Ellis, nationally known psychiatrist and sexologist, if he had been asked, might well have declared that unnecessary restrictions on the sexual life of Americans are partially responsible for our violence. He has noted that frustrations arising from sexual problems often lead to anger and rage which in turn lead to violence, and that the more frustration a person builds up the greater the tendency to violence.

4. Murder. A very large majority of murders occur because of severe and often overwhelming sexual tensions, fantasies, anxieties, and conflicts. Those ancient enemies of man, guilt and fear, prey on the minds of some people sufficiently to incite them to murder. Men taunted by unloving wives about their sexual ability or capacity often turn on their tormenters and kill them. Sadists, who receive sexual gratification from the suffering of others, often commit the most horrible murders. Suppressed homosexuals, because of guilt and fear over their socially condemned condition, erupt in murderous rages and kill their sexual partners. Husbands who discover their wives with other men often kill one or both.

5. *Parental child abuse and child murder.* This is a far greater problem than most of the public suspect. Since hospitals have reported these cases to the police, it has become evident that there are many more child-haters than formerly imagined. The shocking fact is that the cause could be unconscious hatred for sex by the parents. Married couples may be so thoroughly indoctrinated with the idea that sex is evil that they unconsciously consider the child evil because it arrived in this world as a result of their own evil actions. Parents who beat and murder a small child, obviously have an intense hatred of the child, a hatred no child could bring down on its head by its own actions.

6. *Blackmail.* Blackmail, one of the most despicable of crimes, is a demoralizing source of fear to homosexuals. It is a deplorable fact that because of the antihomosexual laws, blackmailers limit their victims almost exclusively to homosexuals. They are quite aware that homosexuals dare not file charges and consequently feel secure in squeezing every cent they can from their helpless victims.

In some cities homosexual blackmail is even practiced by the police. In a speech to the National Prohibition and Parole Association, Kinsey pointed this out, saying, "There are cities in the United States where there is no greater blackmail racket than that operated by the police against homosexuals."

Homosexuality practiced between willing partners is as remotely associated with crime as blackmail is associated with law observance. Yet the blackmailer is actually protected by the laws that make the homosexual vulnerable.

7. *Drug Addiction.* Drugs relax and alleviate the tensions, guilt, frustrations, and fears stirred up by sexual conflicts. In fact, fear of sex may be the dominant factor in most drug addictions. Contrary to the opinion of some, drugs deaden the sex urge and consequently keep the user away from sexual temptations.

Society's brutality toward homosexuals undoubtedly drives many of them to drug addiction. Jesse Stern, in his book *The Sixth Man* (a study of homosexuality), expressed his opinion that many homosexuals in New York were or will become drug addicts.

8. *Alcoholism and drunkenness.* Alcohol, because it acts as a relaxer of inhibitions, frees men of their guilt and fear of sex. One authority actually estimated that 50 percent of men found it necessary to use alcohol as a relaxing agent before having intercourse with their wives. Dr. George Crane, the noted medical columnist, once declared that if it were not for unresolved sexual conflicts, most bars and liquor stores would close for lack of business.

If you could get to the bottom of the trouble with alcoholics, you would probably find sexual conflicts as the root cause.

9. *Divorce.* Sexual incompatability, sexual frustration, sexual guilt, sexual fears, and hatred of sex cause about 95 percent of all divorces. Two of the greatest contributors to sexual guilt and sexual fears are a negative approach to sex and the demand for total abstinence from all types of sexual outlets until marriage. It is a psychological absurdity to have the evils of sex drilled into anyone from childhood until marriage and then to expect a miraculous change to occur on the night of the marriage. For anyone to expect the newly married couple to discard their accumulated unconscious sexual guilt and fears is ridiculous. Only through psychiatric treatment would it be possible to purge the mind of its psychological burdens. Under the circumstances it is amazing that there are not more divorces.

10. *Teenage unrest and delinquency.* This puzzling social problem is primarily caused by the struggle between the natural sex urges of sexually mature teenagers and the impossible restrictions placed on their sexual activity by their elders. As Freud pointed out, many parents are actually jealous of their own children. An explanation for this is an unconscious urge for sexual intercourse with those of the opposite sex, which would be understandable. This is proved by many parents' efforts to prevent teenagers from achieving any theoretical or practical acquaintance with sexuality and by the severe punishment often meted out for excursions into this forbidden field. This could also be the cause of parents raising an uproar about sex education in the schools and the demands that sex education be left to them, which is quite

absurd because most parents probably know even less than their children. Even if they could teach their teenagers the facts, many of them are too ashamed even to mention the subject.

For sexually mature human beings to be placed in the hopeless biological position of forced abstinence from any type of sexual release until marriage is cruel and inhuman treatment. Even uncivilized savages have more wisdom than to attempt this.

Marriage in many parts of the world at the present time occurs shortly after sexual maturity develops at the ages of fourteen to sixteen. People in these regions instinctively follow the natural laws of human sexuality. They are not forced to disobey the sex laws and religious restrictions that most of us hypocritically pretend to support publicly while doing as we please in private. It is not a matter of *wanting* to be hypocrites, but of being *forced* to be so.

Kinsey discovered the dramatic fact that the male in the United States is at the peak of his sexual potency and activity between sixteen and twenty years of age—before he is even married, in most cases. It should be self-evident that *God,* not *man,* determined the natural sexual peak of males. Teenage unrest and delinquency are foregone conclusions under these circumstances.

11. Suicide. Disappointment and despair in love; fear of discovery in sexual involvements producing pregnancy of unmarried females; and, despair of homosexuals because of their cruel persecution by society—all rank as significant causes of suicide.

Thoughtless diatribes by the clergy against the evils of sex can inflict incalculable psychological damage on impressionable and sensitive individuals, often driving them from the church and also causing them to commit suicide.

12. Sexual deviation. Deviations are *unnatural* methods of obtaining sexual gratification. Contrary to the ideas of many people they do not include homosexuality or the use of the erogenous zones, those biological areas placed by nature—in other words by an act of God—to relieve sexual tensions.

In order to understand what a deviation is we should realize that *when a natural biological activity of man is blocked or choked off it will inevitably burst forth into activity at another point.* When the sex urge is blocked through shame, guilt, and fear, it necessarily bursts forth in unusual and even fantastic sexual behavior.

Examples of these deviations are: *sadism*—the torture of human beings, mentally and physically, for sexual gratification; *masochism* —receiving punishment or torture in order to gain sexual relief; *pederasty*—the use of small children for sexual purposes; *necrophilia*—the use of dead bodies for sexual release; *exhibitionism*—exhibition of their sexual organs in public by men to women; and *voyeurism*—peeking.

For religion and sexually ignorant parents literally to drive children to such appalling practices in the hope of saving them from the evils of sex through instilling in their children shame, guilt, and fear of sex constitutes an incredible blunder. The chances are vastly greater that the children will develop as patients for mental hospitals rather than as saints.

13. Homosexuality. This condition—it is neither a disease nor an illness —is a harmless diversion of the sex urge away from the opposite sex to a member of the same sex. The true or genuine homosexual male usually falls in love with another male. The relationship generally quite satisfactory to the individuals concerned if they are left alone by an intolerant society. Psychiatrists believe the root cause of homosexuality is in most cases fear of the opposite sex. Because the exclusive homosexual is usually impotent with members of the opposite sex—in other words unable to have intercourse with them—*there is no alternative for him but sexual association with the same sex,* abstinence being out of the question because it is biologically impossible for sexually healthy individuals.

Dr. William Graham Cole, in his instructive book *Sex and Love in the Bible,* points out the inability of the true homosexual to have sexual relations with the opposite sex:

> The male homosexual incurs fear of the vagina. . . . He *cannot stand it even to insert the penis,* let alone to have an orgasm. This fear of the vagina *makes it necessary* for him to confine his sexual relations to someone of his own sex, someone without the fearful vagina and with the reassuring penis.

Drs. Adelaide Johnson of the University of Minnesota and David Robinson of the Mayo Clinic in Rochester, Minnesota, in a joint study of sexual deviations and their causes, state flatly that *parents are the major basic cause*. They found that parents help develop homosexuality and numerous other sexual deviations in their children because of *a subconscious response to their own sexual frustrations*. All parents of homosexuals and sexual deviates had unhappy and unsatisfactory sex relations. In other words, parents, through their own uncontrolled fears of sex, push their children into the very things they fear themselves.

14. Impotence and frigidity. Impotent men and frigid women are almost always victims of sexual guilt and fear established in their childhood. In the case of men, impotency might be termed symbolic self-castration.

Dr. Abraham Stone, New York urologist and marriage counselor, estimates that 70 percent or more of all impotence has no physical basis. He says, "Such impotent men suffer childhood feelings that sex is wholly evil, nasty, and dirty."

Psychologically, impotence smothers the guilt feelings caused by what the individual considers evil sex activity, consequently making it impossible for him to have successful intercourse.

15. Chronic disorder of the sex glands. This physical disorder is suffered by one-third of all males over thirty-five in the United States because of improper drainage of the sex glands. Sexual arousal causes a seepage of sexual fluids into the ducts leading from the sex glands, which, if left undischarged, undergo chemical changes creating inflammation and deterioration of the healthy tissues. It is plain that the sex glands must be drained as soon as possible so that the seepage may be cleared from the ducts. Because of the numerous ways of arousal, frequent ejaculations are necessary to keep from damaging the sex glands. This fact obviously does not encourage abstinence.

16. Pornography. The United States is noted for its battles against the imaginary evils of pornography, yet, paradoxically, it is also noted for its intense interest in pornography. All that is necessary to make a book a best seller is to condemn it because of its sexual content. For instance the best seller, *Candy*, a much condemned book, sold 140,000 copies in the hardcover edition—this in addition to copies sold in four separate paperback versions in the one year of 1964.

Although psychiatrists tell us that pornographic material has the effect of releasing pent-up sexual tensions and is harmless, many people believe it is evil, causes crimes, and will contaminate their children. Those same children probably learn more harmful sexual habits in back alleys and similar places than they ever could pick up from newsstands and other outlets carrying sexual material.

Pornography is born *only* in the minds of sexually ignorant persons filled with shame, guilt, and fear of their God-given natural sexuality. No one who accepts human sexuality in a natural and realistic manner pays attention to it because to him there is no such thing. As for his neighbors' interests and reading habits in the line of sex, he believes they are neither his business nor the law's concern.

In our crusades against pornography, we pay no attention to the extremely significant psychological fact that human beings, being human beings, *are always intrigued and attracted by the forbidden.* Anything sexual banned by the laws whets the appetite of the the curious. Because it is a challenge, they rush to do the very thing forbidden or condemned. If we need or desire proof of the remarkable lack of interest in pornography when it is not forbidden, Denmark gives us that proof.

In 1967 Denmark threw out its statues on written obscenity and the bottom fell out of the market for pornography. One former publisher complained that books that would ordinarily sell 20,000 copies illegally dropped to about 2,000 to 3,000 when they became legal. *What was no longer forbidden fruit was no longer desirable.* Amazingly, *sex crimes dropped 25 percent* between 1966 and 1967. The population as a whole adopted a more relaxed attitude toward all types of expressing sexuality.

The Danish Permanent Law Committee's secretary, A. A. Brydensholt, reported that "all the experts consulted—psychiatrists, sociologists, criminologists, educators—*all said that there was no proof whatsoever that pornography was a danger to adults or chil-*

dren." Indeed there was no evidence that Danish youth are particularly intrigued by pornography, the customers being primarily adult men.

The report of the Danish Medical-Legal Council was the vital factor in the abolition of the Danish laws on pornography. It amazingly (to those of us who believe pornography is a deadly menace) found that *pornographic material did not cause an increase of sex crimes* (as is charged so often in the United States); that it *did not alter the directions of sexual desires or seriously change sex attitudes by vulgarizing sex* (another charge often made in the United States); it found in general that pornographic material *had no harmful effects*. On June 1, 1969, the Danish Parliament voted to make legal the sale of pictorial pornography, in addition to that of written pornography, to anyone over sixteen (please note—sixteen).

Some illuminating comments were made by a leading producer of pornographic pictures in Denmark, Jens Theander: "The Danes are fed up with porno. It's been legal too long." Imagine, two years of freedom to buy it and they were fed up! "The curious people disappear."

Dr. Anders Groth, psychiatrist in Sakt Hans Hospital, the largest mental hospital in Denmark, predicted, "As soon as the appetite is satisfied the market will dwindle to a very small one." That is exactly what happened. The vast majority of buyers ordered only a few times, and most of them were at least thirty-five years old.

Those who carry on vigorous campaigns to suppress pornography should be made aware that a large percentage of psychologists and psychiatrists (86.1 percent of 3,400 who filled out a University of Chicago poll, the results of which were announced on August 23, 1969) believed persons who wage such campaigns are often *motivated by unresolved sexual problems in their own characters*. In other words, these people are so burdened with feelings of sexual guilt and fear over their own sexual activities that they attempt to appease them by vigorously opposing pornography.

The startling fact is such antipornography campaigners—if they only realized it—are the best promoters, advertisers, and salesmen that pornography dealers could ask for. Human beings, being human, cannot resist the fascinating lure of discovering for them-selves just what the uproar is all about. Forbidden fruit is far more interesting, as the Danes proved, than something easliy attainable, just as watermelons swiped from a watermelon patch taste much better to kids than if they bought them.

Even the naked body causes an uproar among many people, as though it were an evil thing. Nudist magazines and other pub-lications with pictures of naked men and women have recently ap-peared on the newsstands, much to the horror of some of the public. They seem unaware of the biblical quotation from the story of Eve's creation from the rib of Adam and their marital union, which closed with the comment "And the man and his wife were both naked, *and they were not ashamed.*"

Michelangelo, when painting in the Vatican, was condemned for painting his biblical characters in the nude by the cardinals who called the pictures obscene. He answered them by exclaiming, "I will paint man *as God made him, in all the glory of his nakedness.*" If man in his nakedness was *good enough for God* he certainly should be *good enough for us.* How in the name of common sense are we ever going to have respect for ourselves *if we fear and hate our own bodies?*

Most of us are still unaware of the disastrous significance of sexual ignorance. We still unconsciously cling to the ideas instilled in us by Christianity that sex is a hush-hush subject, something to be hidden, something to be whispered about, something never to be mentioned or discussed frankly, something to be feared. Beyond all question, this attitude could *never* lead to a sexually enlightened, educated, and understanding society. You just don't learn anything by never discussing a subject.

Because we have pretended for so long that sex does not exist, our minds may be closed to any suggestion that our unnatural, un-realistic, and fearful sexual attitudes could be the major cause of such social plagues as crime, alcoholism, drug addiction, divorce, murder, suicide, juvenile unrest and delinquency, and the self-evi-dent sexual social problems described in this chapter.

We might as well make up our minds that, when we fight nature, nature will fight back and nature will win because *God and nature are synonymous.* There is not the slightest doubt that when man attempts to change the natural laws of the body according to his own whims or fancies he, and he alone, will reap the consequences of his rash act. *God does not have to punish us. If we disobey the natural laws of the body, we automatically bring down on our own heads our own suffering and pain.*

Too many religious leaders, too many lawmakers, too many law-enforcement officials, and too much of society take it for granted that these problems are the result of the sinfulness and wickedness of man. The thought never occurs to them that they themselves might be causing these social afflictions by attempted enforcement of unnatural sexual restrictions. It never occurs to them that their laws and regulations are attempting the overthrow of the natural laws of the body. It never occurs to them that human error caused by human ignorance of the biological construction of the human body has degraded sexual functioning into an evil instead of the blessing God himself intended.

17. Venereal disease. The spread of venereal disease has reached epidemic proportions nationally, as noted, for example, by *Newsweek* in the article "VD, The Epidemic" (January 24, 1972). Similarly, the *Washington Post,* under the headline "Washington Leading City in VD Cases," reminds us that more people in the Washington area get venereal diseases than mumps, measles, tuberculosis, chicken pox, hepatitis, and whooping cough put together. Washington may lead the major cities in the number of veneral disease cases. The statistics reported suggest that the infection rate is also rising rapidly in the middle class. (In the lower class the rate is high but remains stable.) Venereal disease apparently has extended into a stratum of society where it used to be very rare. Jere Houseworth, chief statistician for the Federal Center for Communicable Disease in Atlanta, reports that "the most prevalent of all communicable diseases, except for the common cold and influenza, in most parts of the country is gonorrhea."

Cases of gonorrhea have reached a record high in the United States, with more than 2.3 million cases estimated. This is an increase of 16 percent over 1969. The U.S. Public Health Service estimated that probably more than half a million Americans are unaware they have syphilis and are in need of help with medical treatment. By not getting medical aid, they risk paralysis, insanity, blindness, and heart trouble. With proper training about sexual relationships, people who get venereal disease will not be afraid or ashamed to get medical treatment as soon as possible. They must overcome feelings of fear and guilt, and get to a doctor or medical aid center at once.

The *Newsweek* article describes attempts by the federal government to bring syphilis under control by case finding. Since 1962, when the U.S. Surgeon General created a major stir about the increasing cases of syphilis, more than 6.3 million dollars have been spent annually, largely to pay case finders. Because the expenditures have not kept pace with inflation, the number of investigators has been trimmed from 800 in 1964 to about 500 today. This, many observers believe, is one reason why syphilis cases rose 8 percent in 1970 and 16 percent in 1971, the largest case load in the twenty years since penicillin came into general use.

So we find the great need to prove to so many teenagers and adults that they must seek medical help as soon as they find they have contracted a venereal disease. It is no disgrace for anyone to seek a doctor's help for any reason whatsoever, as long as he needs help. There are plenty of health centers already established to help those with venereal diseases, or they can go to any doctor. The real disgrace is in ignoring the chance of paralysis, insanity, blindness, and heart trouble by not being treated for venereal diseases. Even more disgraceful is the possibility of passing these diseases on to other people because the victims of the disease have not been treated themselves.

So the best plan seems to be to make it legally possible to treat anyone afflicted with a venereal disease without asking any embarrassing questions. With full assurance that they will not be reported to the police, these people would feel free to seek help either from a health center or a doctor. Under these protective conditions a publicity program could be carried by many news media, geared for a short effective slogan to encourage afflicted people to get treatment at once.

In the living of life, every mind must face the unyielding rock of reality, of a truth that does not bend to whim or fancy, of a rule that measures the life and mind of men.

THOMAS AQUINAS

Human sexuality was obviously created by God for the purpose of perpetuating the human race and populating the world. What some of us do not seem to realize is that God also created sexuality as the natural source from which all love springs, and that he meant it to be a source of pleasure, joy, and happiness.

The idea that God commands us to deprive ourselves of the satisfaction, love, and happiness that sex provides is pure nonsense. For centuries Christianity has attempted and (needless to say, without success) to limit the sex act to the purpose of procreation only. This limitation could have prevented the number of sex acts from exceeding the number of children in the family. In other words, five children would mean sexual intercourse only five times in a lifetime. Can you imagine anything more ridiculous?

As anyone with a good sexual education is aware, the human body, as it is constructed and was created by God, is provided with the ability to release automatically built-up sexual tensions at various intervals, depending on the strength of the individual's sex drive or the rapidity of the bodily manufacture of sexual fluids. For males this may be once a month or from fifteen to twenty times a week, with an average of two or three times a week.

One of the most destructive enemies of American physical and mental health is our appalling lack of factual knowledge of our sexual nature. Not only is the public filled with superstition and ignorance, but so are authorities most often approached by the sexually distressed—the clergy and the medical profession.

We are, in fact, so woefully ignorant that Dr. L. T. Woodward, an outstanding American physician, was moved to write a book with the startling title *Ninety Percent of what You Know About Sex is Wrong.* In it he explodes many of the myths, fancies, and superstitions that cause so much guilt and fear.

Unquestionably, the public lack of knowledge of the basic facts concerning a number of vital sexual activities has contributed greatly to the development of the social problems discussed in chapter 2.

Following are a numbr of the essential sexual facts that everyone should know:

1. Babies are born with and display sexual activity from the time they are born.

Many parents have the false idea that their babies and small children should display no sexuality whatsoever. Any such display often brings unjustified and cruel punishment down on the children's heads and probably introduces unnatural and damaging shame, guilt, and fears into their lives.

Infants are born with and display sexual feelings and desires *according to God's own plan.* Medical authorities have even discovered that a male child sometimes has erections while still in his mother's womb. Even in babyhood, children will instinctively and naturally reach for the parts of their mother's body that excite them most. Their sexual curiosity and sex play is as natural as hunger for food. It certainly is not "dirty" or nasty, and it is not sinful because God Himself provided curiosity so that children might grow and develop sexually. To destroy that curiosity may sexually cripple them for life.

When the child's mother responds with loving warmth, she automatically prepares him for normal and healthy sexual behavior. But if she slaps, scolds, or rejects the child in any way, or recoils in horror at his natural sexual activity, she will quickly make him feel that his actions are bad; she effectively plants the seeds of shame, guilt, and fear that develop into an abnormal and unsatisfactory sex life in the adult.

By the end of the second year, there are definite evidences of the child's sexual life. Parents unaware of this fact assume that the child has no sexual life and no sexual feelings. The child soon learns that he must act externally in accordance with this myth. Dr. Menninger says that one of the most frequent memories uncovered by patients in psychoanalysis is their profound disappointment and bitterness when they come to recognize (often before the age of seven) that their parents indulge in sexual activity forbidden to themselves and represented to them as "bad." Added to this frustration are their guilts caused by the experiences of masturbation and sexual curiosity about the opposite sex, anxiety about the possible loss of the penis by boys, and the assumption by girls that they have been injured or slighted in some way, and, for both boys and girls hostility toward the parent of the same sex. The cure for these problems is a thorough knowledge and understanding of the true sexual nature of man by the parents. Parents who accept sexual love as good, wholesome, and beneficial—not as something evil, to be feared and hated—will automatically impart this attitude to their children, thus preventing them from becoming alcoholics, drug addicts, juvenile delinquents, criminals, or sex perverts. It cannot be emphasized enough that fear of sex is a dreadful and catastrophic evil that only time and a repudiation of ancient religious superstitions and myths can cure.

2. *The sense of touch is important in the sexual development of the child.* The importance of the sense of touch was described by Ashley Montagu in his book *Touching—The Human Significance of the Skin.* Ashley Montagu is an anthropologist interested in bridging the gap between the social and the biological sciences. His career involves teaching at New York University, Harvard, and the University of California as a professor of anatomy and anthropology. He is also the author of thirty books and numerous articles.

His book is a study of the importance of tactile experience in the development of the human being. "Tactile" means of or pertaining to the organs of sense or touch. Skin is considered only as it relates to the sexual activity of human beings. Skin covers the entire body, making it the largest organ in the human body and the most efficient protector.

The sense of touch is directly connected with the skin, and the development of the sensitivities of the skin depends on the kind of environmental stimulation it receives. Touch by the mother in holding and cuddling of the baby has an important and effective part in the later development of the child. As the mother holds the child in a close embrace so the adult will later in life want to be held by and to hold anyone he or she loves to demonstrate his feeling.

If the holding and cuddling is not satisfied in childhood, the lack can carry over into adulthood and, according to a study of thirty-nine women, cause acute psychiatric disorders or relatively acute psychiatric problems. Dr. Marc H. Hollender, of the Department of Psychiatry of the University of Pennsylvania, who made the clinical study of the thirty-nine women, found neurotic depression the most common disorder among them. Twenty-one women of this group had used sex to entice a male to hold them, and twenty-six had made direct requests to be held. It is easily understood that such women may entice men into sex relations when their real physical need is merely to be held or cuddled. One of Hollender's coworkers, Lowen, writes, "This compulsive activity may give the impression these persons are oversexed. They are, if anything, undersexed, because the activity stems from a need for erotic stimulation rather than a feeling of sexual charge or excitement. Sexual activity of this kind never leads to orgastic satisfaction or fullfillment, but leaves the person empty and disappointed." This is just another result of improper sexual training in childhood.

Touch is the means of communication that enables the child to understand that he is being loved. When a child is petted, cuddled, and carried because he is loved, he learns to touch others the same way. In this sense love is sexual and means concern, tenderness, responsibilities, and thinking of the needs of others. This is all communicated through the child's skin in the first months of his life. The messages he receives through the skin must be a feeling of security and pleasure if the child is to develop normally. Ashley Montagu writes, ". . . evidence as we have strongly suggests that inadequate communication with the baby through its skin is likely to result in inadequate development of sexual functions."

During the latency period, girls and especially boys are less likely to seek and receive tactual contacts from parents. At puberty or soon after, tactual sensitivity comes back stronger than ever to become a major need in the search for intimacy, acceptance, and reassurance. If this need has not been fulfilled in childhood, it results in a constant avoidance of intimacy, acceptance, and reassurance with other people.

As Lowen points out, "The quality of the physical intimacy between mother and the child reflects the mother's feelings about the intimacy of sex. If the act is viewed with disgust, all intimate body contact is tainted with this feeling of disgust. Each contact with the child is an opportunity for the child to experience the pleasure of the intimacy or to be repulsed by the fear and shame of it. The child of a mother who is afraid of intimacy will develop a feeling of shame about its own body."

Slapping infants as a form of discipline or otherwise turns the skin into an organ of pain rather than pleasure. This goes against nature and may lead to harder blows and serious injury to the baby.

The female, at all ages, seems to be more responsive to tactuality than the male, who depends more on visual stimulation.

Margaret Mead has said that American mothers tend to be closer to daughters than sons. Many American mothers deliberately understimulate their sons sexually and emotionally, according to the clinical experience of Erickson.

3. Children become sexually mature at twelve to fourteen.

Specifically, this is the age when boys begin ejaculating their sexual liquids and attain the ability to procreate children, and girls begin having their monthly periods and attain the ability to become mothers. In other words, the boy's sexual organs begin manufacturing the sperm to impregnate the girl, and the girl begins to deposit eggs in her womb.

This is the point in human life that nature has provided for the procreation of children; however, civilization, through its advancements and educational system, has made marriage at this age impractical, and therein lies the problem. How are children of this age who were formerly recognized as adults and married shortly after arriving at sexual maturity, going to find the necessary sexual outlets? No one has recognized this fact or provided any socially or religiously acceptable means of relieving their sexual tensions.

Of the three types of sexual outlets—masturbation, homosexuality, and heterosexuality—only masturbation and homosexuality could prevent impregnation of tens of thousands of unmarried girls each year.

Masturbation, which has been condemned in the past as harmful and sinful, is practically a universal practice among human beings. It is in no way harmful and is a natural way to release sexual tensions. All social and religious condemnation of masturbation should cease, and it should become a recognized and accepted way of sexual relief.

Homosexuality, so abhorrent to many people (in public), is widely practiced in the East. Douglas Plummer in his book on homosexuality, *Queer People,* points out:

> In many parts of the East, where sexual passion is regarded as a pleasurable pastime, homosexual practices are regarded as an additional outlet. Homosexual behavior creates no problems and is not regarded as obnormal. . . . I have seen young men and boys walking hand in hand in such cities as Damascus, Aleppo, Beirut, Bagdad, and Tehran. No doubt when they are twenty-two and twenty-three these youngsters will be married, with children. But now, when sixteen or seventeen or more, they enjoy homosexual friendships which are accepted by their parents and by all adults as being quite normal and only to be expected. . . . There is no trace of effeminacy in such relationships, but affection and comradship are constantly present. . . . So there are no homosexual criminals and there is no waste of time of the state and police.

In the United States as elsewhere, homosexuality should be made legal and acceptable for those who desire to practice it. It might at least prevent some of the unwanted pregnancies of unmarried girls and some of the illegal abortions that often cause the death of the girls receiving them.

Let's face it honestly. Man-made laws and religious regulations requiring total abstinence until marriage do not work and have no more chance of working than a snowball has of surviving on the Fourth of July. The natural laws of human sexuality cannot be altered or changed to suit the whims or fancies of man.

4. The sexual needs, demands, and activity of the male reach their peak between the ages of sixteen and twenty.

This startling biological fact was discovered by Kinsey and disclosed over twenty years ago, but society, religion, and the penal authorities have yet to give evidence of recognizing this extremely fundamental fact of human sexuality.

Most males reach and pass this natural sexual peak before they even get married. Amazingly, society and religion seemingly have ignored this condition, having done nothing to change the old rules. There is still not a single acceptable, uncondemned, lawful outlet for the unmarried to relieve their sexual tensions.

As every observing realistic person is aware, masturbation, homosexuality or heterosexuality is indulged in by all healthy males *before* marriage, ignoring every sexual rule, regulation, and law on the books. It is not at all unusual for many males to use all three methods for most of their lives.

God is responsible for human beings reaching sexual maturity at the age of thirteen or fourteen. If social conditions make marriage feasible at twenty-two or twenty-three then the church, the state, and society had better adapt their regulations and laws to the change, and not attempt the impossible task of changing human nature to fit their laws and regulations.

5. Total abstinence from sexual activity would result in atrophy of the sexual muscles and nerves and eventually cause the extinction of man.

Atrophy of any part of the body means that it wastes away and becomes useless. This occurs when that part cannot be used because of injury or some other cause.

Our sexual mechanism is animated by nerves and muscles that must be exercised or they will atrophy and become unusable. If nature had not seen to it that the sex drive was so powerful that it could not possibly be blocked, the ten years, more or less, of abstinence, demanded by religion and the legal codes between sexual maturity and marriage would have been disastrous to the human race.

God in his infinite wisdom created the sex drive so powerful that man, no matter how ignorant and stupid his sexual beliefs and laws, could not possibly cause the destruction of the human race.

6. *The sex drive is the motivating force of human life, making human beings sexual beings.*

Whether we are horrified or not, the inescapable fact is that the sex urge is the core of life, the hub of our existence, the source from which flow all the finer characteristics of man, including love, tenderness, affection, devotion, and sympathy.

Sexual intercourse, when used as a means of expressing love, is the finest and most wonderful of all methods of showing devotion and affection. It may also be a matter of friendship between two individuals mutually atracted. Biological sexual demands make sexual intercourse or some other method of relieving sexual tensions an inevitable and unavoidable physical and mental requirement for good health and the living of a full life.

Medical authorities long ago found that the entire body is attuned to and responds to sexual stimulation. In other words, our entire body is sexual—we are sexual beings. The human nervous system—as God designed it and willed it to be—is one single network extending throughout the entire body; consequently, proper stimulation of just one part of that system commonly produces sexual responses in all the other parts. In fact, proper stimulation in any part of the body in many people will produce an orgasm. If that is not enough, all of the senses—sight, hearing, smell, touch, and taste, as God destined them to be—are natural stimulators of the sex urge. Even any associations of ideas derived from the individual's sexual experiences act as unconscious and automatic stimulators.

How can there be any possible doubt that humans are sexual beings?

7. *The erogenous zones used in anal and oral intercourse are equipped by nature as sexual zones.*

The human body—by the will of God—is equipped with special zones possessing great sexual sensitivity and known as erogenous zones. They are—probably to the horror and amazement of those who imagine their use to be "crimes against nature"—the anus, lips, mouth, tongue, breast, and, of course, the genitals.

Each of these areas, whose use has falsely been termed "perversions" or "deviations" or "crimes against nature," possesses a heavy concentration of sexually sensitive nerve endings, making them especially fitted for sexual use. Unquestionably, human beings have nothing whatsoever to do with the placing of these zones in their bodies.

In spite of society's condemnation of the use of anal and oral intercourse, it has been estimated that fully half of the married couples in this country practice one or all of these methods of sexual gratification. Yet punishment for the use of these God-created zones is cruel and inhuman. How can such uses honestly be called "crimes against nature" when nature itself provided for these zones for sexual purposes?

Amazingly, too, they provide a perfectly natural means of birth control, yet because of religious scruples and legal prohibitions that fact is not recognized, at least publicly. There is no doubt that millions of Americans do use anal and oral intercourse as a natural means of birth control, secretly, in the privacy of their bedrooms. The only possible way of enforcing the present laws against these practices would be to station a policeman under every bed in the country, which is of course ridiculous.

8. *The replenishing of sexual liquids is a continuous bodily process in males.*

It seems that much of society is unaware that, in the male, the filling of the sex glands with sexual liquids is a continuous biological process which neither religion nor the law can block or control. Full sex glands automatically create nervous sexual tensions that demand release in an ejaculation just as the bladder becomes full and demands drainage. This endless glandular activity continues throughout much or all of life.

Dr. Wilhelm Reich declares, "One does not have sexual intercourse in order to have children, but because fluid congestion produces a bioelectric charge in the genital organs and presses for discharge."

In connection with this fact, many of us have the false belief that males can damage themselves by too much sexual indulgence. In *Ninety Percent of what You Know about Sex Is Wrong,* Dr. L. T. Woodward states, "The only thing too much sexual indulgence can lead to is fatigue." He goes on to explain that the male body is equipped by nature with a built-in safety mechanism to prevent overindulgence beyond a healthy point. When the individual personal limit is reached (it varies greatly in individuals), nothing more serious than physical weariness sets in.

This might be explained in another way. When a male supply of semen is drained, his desire for further indulgence ends, just as in urination, when the bladder is empty, the need to urinate disappears. By the very nature of his bodily processes, the male requires a period of time for his body to manufacture a new supply of liquids. The length of time necessary for his particular body determines his need for release of his sexual tensions through sexual indulgence. It may be once a day, once a week, or once a month.

9. The production of sperm is a continuous process after the arrival of sexual maturity.

Many sexually ignorant people still imagine that a male's supply of sperm is permanently exhausted by too much sexual indulgence. A recent religious pamphlet seen by the author condemned masturbation and evidently attempted to frighten boys with the tale that, by indulging in it, they would exhaust their supply of semen and lose their ability to create children. This is an appalling example of what some religious leaders know about human sexuality.

The truth is that at each ejaculation—provided that the ejaculations do not come too close together—the truly amazing number of 500,000 sperm are expelled from the testes. And mind you—just a single sperm is required to fertilize the female egg.

Nature itself provided for the rapid expulsion of sperm by sexual indulgence, for it is now known that they deteriorate and die of old age if they are allowed to accumulate in the testes for too long a period.

10. Animal sex instincts are not comparable with the human sex drive.

Human sexuality is as different from animal sexual instincts as day is from night. Human sexuality makes human beings sexual beings. It is the source of all love—provided it is not smothered by the domination of the self-preservation drive. It is through sexual intercourse that love is renewed and invigorated—if we have the proper sexual attitudes. Every feeling of love, affection, and tenderness has its origin in the sex drive. All religion, art, music, architecture, and in fact, every activity in which the improvement of the environment and welfare of the human race is the goal have their origins in the sex drive.

To compare human sexuality with animal sex, to call it base, or bestial, or part of our lower nature, is an insult to God. Man, and man alone, through his sexual ignorance, his unrealistic attitudes, his superstitions and his unnatural and irrational fears of sex, turns it into a base, or vile, or bestial activity.

Sex in the animal world is for just one purpose—reproduction. It is never an act of love and it does not renew and invigorate love. It is simply a means of producing offspring for the preservation of the species. To believe that human sexuality exists on the same level as the mating of animals is absurd.

Humans, although they may be animals, are much superior and different animals. Humans have a soul—animals do not; humans have intelligence and reasoning powers—animals do not; humans have the ability to love—animals do not; humans have an instinctive urge to worship their creator—animals do not; human sexuality is the hub around which human life is centered—animal sexual activity is for prolonging the species. In other words, human sexuality is the distinguishing characteristic that makes human beings human beings.

For many centuries Christian sexual beliefs were based on the false premise that the purpose of sex was reproduction and reproduction only. Under no circumstances was it to be indulged in otherwise. Presumably, and perhaps without realizing it, human observation of animal sexual activity furnished the basis for believing that human sexual activity was the same. As civilization advanced, many anatomical discoveries were inevitably made, many of them only recently—in fact within the last fifty years. Lacking this knowledge, the early Christians religious authorities had only the Bible and their own very limited sexual knowledge and theories on which to base their sexual laws and regulations.

Today we have sufficient biological and psychological knowledge to prove that sex in humans has a multipurpose function. As usual, human reluctance to abandon old superstitions and myths and to accept new scientific facts has prevented the adoption of new sex laws and regulations in harmony with the latest sexual knowledge. Too many religious leaders cling stubbornly to the old disapproved theories for fear of losing face; they simply refuse to face the facts. Others simply cannot be bothered to take the time to acquaint themselves with the latest knowledge on this most vital of human functions.

The human body only functions properly when it functions as God created it to function and is its own best proof of God's will. If we persist in defying the natural laws of human sexuality, we will inevitably suffer the consequences in divorce, crime, drug addiction, alcoholism, and the rest of the demoralizing social problems we seem unable to solve.

11. Female sexual nature is biologically adaptable to male sexual needs.

Probably one of the greatest causes of divorce is the failure of women to recognize and understand the fact that the release of sexual tensions in the male is a biological requirement necessary for his physical and mental well-being. Biologically, he is created to manufacture sexual liquids automatically in his sex glands. The pressure of these liquids must be released by expulsion as rapidly as the glands become full, whether it be once a week, once a day, or more often. His requirements are determined by his individual capacity. He is therefore not demanding sexual intercourse simply because he enjoys it but because he must function sexually as God created him to. On the other hand, he is limited in his sexual requirement for the same reason.

The healthy female has no such limitations, having an unlimited capacity for sex because she is not dependent on a supply of liquids. She is able to have intercourse once or a dozen times a day. If this were not true, female prostitutes would be physically unable to take care of customers in almost unlimited numbers.

The sexual incompatibility of most married people is wholly uncalled for because female sexual nature is naturally adaptable to most male sexual requirements whatever they may be. Unfortunately, many females are so inhibited by sexual fears, sexual ignorance, and religious scruples that they drive their husbands into adultery, homosexuality, or to prostitutes. Then if a husband's straying is discovered by his wife, she usually demands a divorce, never realizing that it is she who has driven her husband to these outlets by her refusal to provide for his needs. Men can also, by their crude and clumsy methods, make sexual intercourse unsatisfying and burdensome to their wives instead of a pleasure. Often, because of unconscious fears and guilt, they do little more than relieve themselves of their sexual liquids, with little thought of their wives' satisfaction.

Someone has said that a woman must be two things to satisfy a normal man in marriage: a good sex partner and someone who does not nag. Companionship and sex are the first two essential requirements to make a man's home life satisfactory and happy, but it has been found that women consider companionship and sex no better than fifth and sixth in importance in marriage. This fact discloses a wide gap between men and women and explains the breaking up of so many homes. In fact, one authority has estimated that 75 percent of marriages are foredoomed because of sexual incompatibility. No woman can expect her husband to change his biologically determined sexual nature to suit her whims and fancies. The belief that sex is only for the purpose of having children, or a necessary evil to be endured, will soon break up a family. God created the female to adapt herself to the sexual needs or requirements of the male; biologically, therefore, there is no need for sexual incompatibility in most cases.

12. The great variations in sexual capacity and behavior are astonishing.

The public as a whole shows little realization of the fact that human beings display phenomenal variations in sexual behavior and capacity. Unfortunately, religion has based its regulations and legislators have based their laws on the assumption that we were all cast in the same mold, that we have identical sexual capacities and the ability to behave sexually in the same way.

Medical science itself is unable to establish what is normal. The individual desires and capabilities from adolescence to old age cannot be determined by the size of the body, or by the size of the sex organs, or by intelligence, strength, or age. All factors relating to sex show extraordinary individual variations; consequently, each individual has his own unique sexual problems.

As Kinsey observes, "The publicly pretended code of morals, our social organizations, our marriage customs, our sex laws, and our educational and religious systems are based on the assumption that individuals are much alike sexually, and that it is an equally simple matter for all of them to confine their behavior to a single pattern which the mores dictate."

It is quite understandable why we hypocritically pretend to support our impossible sex laws without the slightest idea of obeying them. The truth of the matter is that we could not obey them if we wanted too. God alone determined human sexuality; they are not determined by man-made sex laws and regulations. There is nothing incredible or puzzling or mysterious about the failure of sex laws or of religious prohibitions. The real mystery is why anyone with common sense and intelligence could expect *anything except* sexual confusion, frustration, doubts, tensions, and fears. When we return to obedience of the natural laws and let our natural sexual instincts work instead of choking them off, then, and then alone, will we bring sexual order out of the present sexual chaos.

Puritanical and intolerant sex-haters often have weak sex drives and have no conception of the sexual necessities of those with moderate or strong sex drives. If they are in influential positions or can influence the passing of sex laws, or influence the religious attitudes of people regarding sex, they exercise their power to obtain laws and regulations suitable to their own sexual tastes, with no regard to those with strong sex drives. They seem incapable of realizing that to judge others by their own potential and desires is to perpetrate an outrageous injustice.

Attempting to chain the sex drive in a straightjacket of ineffective laws and regulations can only lead to excessive anxiety, frustration, and despair. But these are not the most serious results. Scientists have found also that *denial of a natural function of the human body almost invariably creates an obsessive concern with the thing denied.* Or we might put it this way: *the more we bottle up the sexual impulses, the harder they fight back.* Following this psychological principle, the inevitable conclusion is that the more religion and the laws attempt to restrict the natural sexual functions, the more people will become obsessed with sex, and the less chance there will be of positive regulation and control of its genuine evils.

In the United States, the state has combined with the church and made every effort to restrict the indulgence in sex to an absolute minimum. Today we are reaping a harvest of sexual rebellion by the young, who have acquired enough sexual knowledge to know that sex is definitely nothing to be ashamed of, feel guilty about, or to hate. They just cannot see how a natural function of the human body can be as evil as their elders proclaim it is. Unfortunately, the sexual pendulum is swinging to exhibitionism, promiscuity, and other genuine sexual evils. Prohibition, as of alcoholic beverages, is not the answer. Reasonable, sensible, natural, and positive regulation and control, plus reasonable, sensible, natural, and positive sexual education is the answer.

No one with common sense and intelligence would even attempt to put out a raging fire by pouring gasoline on it. Yet American society has, in effect, by its attitudes and restrictions, been pouring gasoline on the fires of sexual passion, creating a fantastically obsessive concern with all things sexual.

4   *Sex Drive Neutralizer of Aggression and Violence*

The truth shall make you free.   JESUS CHRIST

The two basic life principles that rule the lives of all human beings, but which unfortunately are generally unknown to the American public, are the sex drive and the self-preservation drive. In the sex drive we find all the virtue and goodness of man; in the self-preservation drive, we find all the aggression and violence. In other words, the good side of man is in his sexuality, the bad side in his struggle for self-preservation.

The incredible fact is that we are not simply good and bad of our own free will, for man's sexuality has not been allowed to operate in man as God designed it to. The real evil has been not in human sexuality but in its *suppression*.

Christianity, by its suppression of the sex instinct, has ignorantly destroyed the power of the sex drive as a natural balancer and neutralizer of the natural aggression and violence inherent in the self-preservation drive.

When God planned the human race He did not limit human sexuality to the purpose of perpetuating man through sexual intercourse, but—equally as important—he provided for it to be the magnet of love and affection which is required to draw the two sexes together in order that they can create children. In addition, the sex drive provides the desire for children and the essential love necessary to nourish and protect them.

The self-preservation drive was created and designed by God not for the purpose of making man evil but for the purpose of furnishing each human being with the weapons (the aggressive characteristics) necessary for his self-defense—for his protection against the perils of life. In other words, it provides the will to act agressively to preserve life, liberty, and happiness. Without it man would vanish from the face of the earth.

Dr. Blanton explains that we must distinguish between hate and normal healthy aggression. Our real problem, he says, is not the aggression itself but the unconscious fear and guilt resulting from false attitudes regarding our aggression. This damaging guilt breeds neurotic hate, which develops into destructive fantasies, forcing us into irrational actions. The love that flows from our sexual nature—providing it is a healthy, natural, and uninhibited love—teaches us to accept our aggressive impulses as normal, and thus frees us from guilt.

Further, guilt over our aggressive feelings impels us to set excessively high goals, goals that are impossible to meet. If we are excessively severe with ourselves, we unconsciously will be excessively severe with everyone we come in contact with. Normal self-love or self-respect is a positive necessity for good health. With it, we avoid neurotic self-criticism, have respect for ourselves, and therefore respect for those with whom we associate.

Christianity, by its constant dwelling on the negative, has committed the cardinal psychological error of forcing us to hate ourselves. Not only do many clergymen harp constantly on man's sinful nature, they preach ceaselessly about God's awful punishment, automatically instilling in us irrational shame, guilt, fear, and self-hatred. And self-hatred can lead only to violence. They set up standards so high the angels themselves would give up in despair. They create religious fanatics who are a scourge to all around them. Somehow, somewhere, they have forgotten or abandoned the words and example of Jesus Christ Himself. They use not realism, not logic, nor common sense. Self-satisfied, they abandon the use of the brains and intelligence God gave them for "suitable" quotations from the Bible, acting as if God Himself had written it and handed it down from heaven. It never seems to dawn on them that we are followers of Jesus Christ and worship him, not the Bible; at least, we pretend we are followers of Jesus Christ. Chesterton voiced a great truth that is impossible to ignore: "Christianity has not failed, because it has never been tried."

In the words of Thomas a Kempis, we find a most appropriate rebuke to those clergymen who attempt to terrorize their congregations into sainthood:

Man thou art, and not God; thou art flesh, not an angel. How can'st thou continue in the same state of virtue, when this was wanting in the angels in heaven and to the first man in paradise?

We have enough problems as human beings without going to church to hear the pastor give psychologically damaging hell-and-damnation sermons. Many of us are already besieged by so many unnatural and irrational fears that only a psychiatrist could help us. It is criminal to fill people with uncalled-for guilt and fear. Most people do the best they know how, which is all God, in his mercy, compassion, and forgiveness, ever expects of us, no matter what the clergy expect. The church, after all, as Cole says, "is not a club for saints but a hospital for sick souls." People go to church for reassurance, consolation, and understanding, *not to be put on the torture rack.* Can you blame so many of them for going fishing instead of to church?

If we become acquainted with the self-preservation drive and its place in the behavior of human beings, we can easily understand that, by using unnatural and irrational shame, guilt, and fear, we automatically force the emergence of aggression, violence, and, eventually, rebellion. It is psychological idiocy to attempt to force human beings to "be good" with these diabolical instruments of psychological demoralization. We would without doubt be a much healthier and happier nation if clergymen of all denominations were required to become practical psychologists as well as clergymen. A minister or priest without a knowledge of human nature is like a doctor without a knowledge of medicines. Jesus knew human nature; undoubtedly he was the greatest psychologist the world has ever known.

Since sexuality has in the past been a devil to be exorcised by Christianity—we imagine much to the dismay of Jesus, who did not hesitate to associate with sexual sinners, and clearly considered them human beings, not beasts—it might be elightening, especially to the clergy, to learn that our sexual nature is the source of all love, pleasure, generosity, tenderness, compassion, mercy, and justice. *Every creative activity of man originates in the sex drive.* All religion—yes, religion itself—originated in human sexuality, horrible as it may seem to those religious people who believe sex is an invention of the devil. All art, architecture, music, literature—in fact, every activity in which the improvement of the environment and welfare of the human race is the goal—originated in human sexuality. All the noble characteristics of man are sexual in nature; we are, unequivocally, sexual beings.

The other side of man's nature is his self-preservation drive, in which—shocking as it may be to the clergy and most of us who believe the evil in man is inspired by Satan or is part of man's inherited evil nature—originate all aggression, violence, hostility, animosity, malice, selfishness, hatred, and like characteristics. They are, surprisingly, weapons of self-defense provided by God to enable man to discourage his enemies and protect him from the dangers he must face in life. They are the weapons he uses when his safety, his freedom, his property, his loved ones, and his life are endangered or threatened.

They are indeed evils, if left to reign unchecked and used without being neutralized, balanced, and controlled by the love originating in the sex drive—providing that love is not smothered and blocked by unnatural sexual attitudes, unnatural sexual "religious" prohibitions, and unnatural sexual laws.

We were created with two basic life principles by God, and *these must be allowed to operate as God designed them to. The balance of nature must be preserved and the natural laws must be obeyed lest we destroy ourselves. In other words, the sex drive must be allowed to control the excesses of the self-preservation drive.*

The ancient belief that we all inherit our evil natures from Adam and Eve, and that we each and every one of us is being punished for a sin committed thousands of years ago by two people we had no connection with and have no proof ever existed, just does not stand up. Collectively, we do not have a sinful nature. Our nature becomes evil only when we destroy the balance between the sex drive and self-preservation drive.

In many babies, who, naturally, cannot reason, we can observe the effects of the self-preservation drive before it is curbed and controlled through love. A baby is born into what is, to it, a strange and terrifying world. Even its parents appear to it as giants who it fears may destroy it. It proves its fears first only by crying but later on also by its destructiveness. It tears up everything it gets its hands on. It bites and hits the people around it. It pounds the dog and drags it around by the tail. In order to control this aggression, the parents must cuddle the baby, love it, and give it constant attention and reassurance. In other words, they must control and balance their self-preservation drive by love. Parents whose sexual love has degenerated into a thing of fear and hatred are utterly incapable of giving the child the love necessary to control its aggressive instincts.

Our society is filled with people whose self-preservation drive has never been neutralized through love—people who have little love or who even are incapable of love. (It is pure ignorance for the clergy to imagine that people can learn to love through sermons on love. After two thousand years of preaching love, the world is still filled with hate. Two thousand years of failure should at least make the clergy *aware* that something is radically wrong.) Such people are known as personality deviates; they kill without compunction. They are the viciously violent criminals. Many of them were probably rejected by their parents or felt they had been rejected. And there is nothing—positively nothing—that is more demoralizing to a child than to feel it is not wanted by its parents.

In order to place human sexuality in a position to neutralize and control the destructive aggressions of the self-preservation drive and attain the balance nature intended, we must accept it as a God-given blessing instead of a satanic evil; we must discard our unnatural and unrealistic attitude that sex in itself is evil (*anything* can be used evilly); and we must learn the true facts of sexual biology and modern psychology.

In the extremely significant words of James E. Payne in *You Can't Run Away From Sex:*

> Most of our incredible state of [sexual] confusion and cross purposes has arisen from a fundamental error: The artificial separation of "sex" from "love." Even the most misguided fanatic can find no fault with the concept of love. No one who has felt even the faint stirrings of gentleness and tenderness, the inward

melting that is a telltale sign of love, can ever doubt the goodness of love. It is the universal basis of religion, the essence of religious feelings, the quintessence of all that is noble within us. It is the only quality that has been made equivalent with God; "God is love." It is the only quality that has lifted man above a mere animal, and made him human.

Yet the sexual urge from which all love derives has been cursed through the ages. . . . Fear of healthy sexual functioning makes healthy sexual functioning difficult or impossible, and when sexual functioning is blocked, the energy converts into anxiety or hostility. And the person who is anxious or hostile tends to fear or hate healthy sexual functioning in others—and the circle continues: what we fear or hate, we pass on to our children, we inflict on our neighbors, we defend in ourselves."

Dr. Blanton, in a strikingly beautiful and informative description of healthy sexual functioning learning without shame, guilt, or fear, explains it in *Love or Perish:*

Of all nature's devices for achieving balance among the forces of life, surely none is a more wonderful creation than the division of mankind into male and female. . . . One need only to imagine its absence to become acutely aware of the overwhelming grandeur with which it carries out nature's basic design.

For it is in joyful union of a man with woman that the jangled forces of life fall at last into harmony. Here, in the eternal longing of one to join with the other, we may discern an infinite wisdom distilled from billions of years of patient evolution. Here lies the primordial pattern of all of our striving and all our bliss. It is the secret spring that animates our deepest desires and shapes our loftiest dreams. It generates the restless tension, the driving energy, that moves us to aspire and achieve. From its profound yearning comes all creation, whether of the body or spirit.

Indeed, "the truth shall make you free."

Homosexuality is assuredly no advantage, but it is nothing to be ashamed of, no vice, no degradation, it cannot be classified as an illness; we consider it to be a variation of the sexual function produced by a certain arrest of sexual development. Many highly respected individuals of ancient and modern times have been homosexuals, several of the greatest men, among them [Plato, Michelangelo, Leonardo da Vinci]. It is a great injustice to persecute homosexuality as a crime, and cruelty too. . . .

FREUD

The homosexual is just another human being who happens to prefer having sexual relations with a member of the same sex instead of the opposite. He is neither dangerous to society or a threat to the public welfare. He neither molests children nor attacks women. In fact, a woman is safer with a homosexual than with a heterosexual. If left alone by a tolerant society to live their lives in their own way, most homosexuals function as normal human beings. *Their only crime is in being different.*

In the United States, the lot of the male homosexual has been a great human tragedy. He has been hated, tormented, persecuted, unprotected by the law, beaten, robbed, blackmailed, driven to suicide, and even murdered—and all because his sexual patterns differ from that of the majority.

We are alleged to be a Christian nation, but who ever heard of Jesus Christ by word or example, persecuting *any* minority with the savagery that the United States has persecuted its homosexuals. Christ taught love, compassion, mercy, and justice, not persecution, intolerance, assault, robbery, and blackmail.

Undoubtedly the guilt and fear forced on the homosexual by society, religion, and the penal laws are his most damaging afflictions. Sometimes they twist and distort his personality until it is literally impossible for him to function as a normal human being. This is the terrible punishment he receives for using the only method of relieving his sexual tensions that he is psychologically capable of. Who is the criminal, the homosexual or society?

If you can, put yourself in his place and answer these questions honestly:

What would *you* do is you were forced to live a life of constant fear and tension?

What would *you* do if your liberty was threatened by arrest and imprisonment every day of your life? (Enforced or not, every law in the penal code against homosexuality is a constant threat to the homosexual's freedom.)

What would *you* do if the horror of public exposure of your private sexual habits and public prosecution were a constant threat?

What would *you* do if the sex laws made it open season on you for blackmailers who, in effect, are protected by the very laws that make you a criminal?

What would *you* do if you were constantly threatened with public humiliation, harassment, and assault by homosexual haters and baiters?

What would *you* do if you were forced to fear every new acquaintance you made because he might take advantage of your criminal status in the eyes of the law to assault and rob you?

What would *you* do if your minister or priest was a homosexual-hater and treated you as some kind of monster doomed to hell?

What would *you* do if you labored under the constant fear that your parents would discover your homosexuality and disown you?

What would *you* do if you were burdened with the constant fear that your heterosexual friends would discover you were a homosexual and ignore you from then on, or even report you to the police?

Is it any wonder that homosexuals become the harassed victims of numerous fears and often become disturbed and neurotic personalities?

WHAT IS A HOMOSEXUAL?

Is he a criminal? Is he a sinner? Is he a monster doomed to hell? Is he mentally unbalanced? Is he a willful and perverse personality using a condemned sexual activity just to be contrary? Does he spread homosexuality like a plague? Is he a child-molester?

Certainly not. Homosexuality is neither a vice nor a disease nor a habit that can be acquired and stopped when desired. Nor is it a practice that can be caught or spread or picked up at school like the chicken pox or measles; nor dirty or wicked or sinful.

Scientifically and medically there is *nothing unnatural* about homosexuality, nor is there anything strange about it because it has been known since man's earliest history. In simple terms, it is the development of man's natural homosexual potential into full homosexuality because of his early environment. However, there may be other causes, and some authorities believe it is congenital.

God Himself, when He created us, provided a homosexual component in us so that we could understand and get along with our own sex.

Charles Berg and Clifford Allan, in their realistic and frank book, *The Problem of Homosexuality,* point out:

> Although the term "homosexuality" applies specifically to behavior, there exists a homosexual component in all living organisms and that its various indirect [non-sexual] forms of expression have a great deal to do with the cohesion of society.

Albert Ellis says that every human being at birth possesses bisexual qualities, that is, characteristics of both the male and female, and thus there is in each one homosexual potentialities.

Berg, whose accomplishments established his reputation as one of the world's great authorities on sexual abnormalities, believed that homosexuality is the result of a combination of a natural biological component plus environmental factors. He wrote:

> My conclusion is that the argument about whether homosexuality is "congenital" or "acquired" is based on misconception. The truth is that "congenital" and "acquired" are different operational stages of the selfsame process, and the one has no meaning without the other, thus, I am convinced that homosexuality, like everything else is both congenital and acquired, with relative quantitative variations of each etiological factor.

The emergence of homosexuality in a person is an indication

that the heterosexual path was blocked, usually by environmental factors, thus allowing the homosexual element to take over. The homosexual, therefore, is *not* a person with a wicked or perverse wish to behave differently from others; he is sexually crippled in the same way as a dwarf—because he has never developed.

Homosexuality can be compared to a seed that sprouts and grows if the necessary environmental elements are present, but stays dormant if these elements are lacking. Unfortunately, sexually ignorant parents, through their own sexual guilt and fears, provide the necessary environment for the homosexual to grow.

The homosexual, then, is *forced* into homosexuality *without his knowledge.* He has no choice in the matter, just as he has no choice of parents. Thus he cannot be blamed for his homosexuality. He becomes aware of it only when he discovers his homosexual desires on the arrival of sexual maturity. He then recognizes the sad fact that the only way he can obtain sexual satisfaction and release from sexual tensions—and at the same time escape from his unconscious fear of the opposite sex—is by sexual relationship with his own sex.

Why does he fear the opposite sex? Cole, as mentioned, says that the major cause of homosexuality in the male is fear of the female vagina. In other words, he has unconsciously acquired a castration complex and pictures the female sex organ as an instrument of castration. Thus, an unconscious fear of losing his penis forces him into homosexuality.

To attempt to force homosexuals to abstain, since they cannot have satisfactory heterosexual relations, can be termed nothing less than cruel and inhuman. There is no greater agony than that endured by the male when he is in extreme desire, his body tense with passion and no release in sight.

Can a true or confirmed homosexual be changed to a heterosexual?

The frank truth is that the true or confirmed homosexual cannot be cured. To talk about curing him is wishful thinking and without a doubt impracticable. To "cure" him you would have to change him into a heterosexual personality. By the time he thinks of going to a psychiatrist, his mental and physical sex habits have become so well established that no amount of treatment can uproot them and replace them with new habit patterns. Even if it were possible, the psychological damage inflicted to his personality in the process might outweigh whatever advantages he might gain from a cure. The cure might indeed be worse than the disease.

The realistic and sensible solution for the homosexual is treatment by a psychiatrist so he could be freed of the guilt and fear caused by a hostile and intolerant society. When he learns to accept himself as he is, he can face his problems with courage.

On this point the *British Medical Journal* for September 15, 1950, quotes Drs. Curran's and Whitby's contributions to the famous "Wolfenden Report":

> The most likely and valuable affects of treatment will be helping the young man whose homosexuality is transient but who requires psychotherapy to help him past it. For the patient who is adjusted to being a homosexual, much less is possible. No doctor could produce for the committee a "cured" case of complete homosexuality.

Havelock Ellis says that he did not have "any knowledge of a case of congenital or fixed inversion in which a complete or permanent transformation has been achieved by psychoanalysis or other psychotherapeutic method."

Berg asserts:

> The fully established practicing male homosexual will never be turned into a heterosexual person. One can say that he may be taught, or teach himself, to do the tricks, but very soon it will be revealed that they are only tricks without substance to them, and he will find himself totally impotent—except with males.

Dr. Stanley Jones writes, in the *Royal Society of Medicine Symposium on Homosexuality:*

> There can be no question of asking the invert to accept the ordinary standards of heterosexual morality, and any course of therapy which seeks to reverse the fundamental pattern is not only foredoomed to failure, as all reported cases testify, but is

also quite indefensible when regarded in the light of absolute morality: attempted "treatment" or alteration of the basic personality of an inborn homosexual can only be described as a moral outrage.

For ministers or priests to expect homosexuals to reform by persuasion or exhortation is worse than useless. Dr. Donald J. West, author of *The Other Man,* writes:

> Religious exhortations, which place emphasis on the wickedness of yielding to impulse, encourage continuance by building up inhibitions based on guilt feelings. If the result were a calm, deliberate decision to behave chastely, it would not be unhealthy, but injudiciously expressed religious precepts tend to exaggerate the sufferer's sense of guilt and shame. Instead of strong-minded self-control, this leads to great misery and to desperate attempts to deny the very existence of the offending impulses. The repression and mental conflicts so provoked may turn the individual into a worse social nuisance and misfit than he would have been if he had simply stayed homosexual.

Unfortunately, this is just what happens in the United States. Our antihomosexual laws and the attitude of religion for the most part force homosexuals into being "a worse social nuisance and misfit."

Dr. Lewis L. Robbins, psychiatrist and medical director at Hillsdale Hospital, points out, in *Why Report:*

> Many homosexuals do not have neurotic conflicts. Their problem is society, because if society would leave them alone, there would be no problem. Many of these do not want to change, and they do not need to change because their behavior is a solution to a problem which is not necessarily disabling. . . . In other words, homosexuality need not impose any limitations on life whatsoever. A man may have another man as a sexual partner, and live without anxiety.

In the many countries where homosexuality is not a crime (even England has had the common sense and wisdom to make it legal), homosexuals betray few if any of the neurotic traits of character found among their counterparts in the United States. The psychologically devastating guilt and fear, the destructive self-hatred often projected to other homosexuals and their enemies, the extreme sensitiveness—even the debasing exhibitionism exhibited by some as a measure of defiance—are all generated by the persecution of a cruel and intolerant society and the threat posed by antihomosexual laws, no matter how hopelessly ineffective and unenforceable. The real crime is not that of homosexuality. It is the crime of an ignorant and superstitious society that has no business prying into the private sexual lives of homosexuals, just as it has no business prying into the private sexual lives of any persons.

It is the total ignorance of most people concerning the true nature of homosexuality that causes most of the trouble for homosexuals. Their only desire is to live their own lives, in their own way, in private, free from persecution and prosecution.

ARE ALL THOSE WHO INDULGE IN HOMOSEXUALITY HOMOSEXUALS?

It is the custom to inaccurately label all those who indulge in homosexuality as homosexuals whether they turn to this method of sexual relief once, several times, or exclusively. Heterosexuals who simply are not repelled by or have no inhibitions regarding the practice of homosexuality and have a strong sex drive often use this method to release their sexual tensions. Especially in cases where wives do not satisfy their sexual needs, some men find relief in homosexual contacts rather than risk extramarital heterosexual affairs. To label such persons homosexuals would be comparable to labeling all drinkers of alcoholic beverages alcoholics simply because they take a drink occasionally.

Most true homosexuals never have sexual intercourse with women. Actually they are repelled by women; they love persons of their own sex, showing in private all the affection and tenderness of heterosexual lovers. Although many homosexuals live together for long periods or even for life, most do not, however, because of their feelings of guilt and this fear of social condemnation and persecution.

The public believes there is a natural instinctive revulsion against homosexuality. Cultural anthropology proves this belief false. Many cultures are tolerant of it and in some cases encouraged it. Most cultures neither encourage it nor punish it, accepting the simple fact that all people are not alike.

Probably the most sensible and realistic classification of those who indulge in homosexuality is that of Dr. Sando Rado, the director of the New York Psychoanalytic Institute. He lists three basic patterns of homosexual behavior: the reparative, the situational, and the variational.

The *reparative* patterns are caused by early sexual fears that inhibit normal sexual functioning in an individual. Reparative acts, mostly unconscious, attempt to repair the damage inflicted on the individual's self-esteem by his sexual failure. Modified forms of sexual activity thus become necessary, and the individual adopts homosexuality. The homosexuality then becomes rigid and inflexible because it is essential to sexual gratification. Those who manifest this behavior are the true homosexuals.

Situational patterns are caused by lack of normal sexual outlets. Heterosexuals, under these circumstances, will seek homosexual outlets. This alternative is a result of conscious choice (the homosexual has no choice) rather than of unconscious necessity. As soon as normal outlets are available, the person abandons his homosexual outlets. No better example can be found than in the American prisons and jails, where many heterosexuals easily shift to homosexuality during the time of imprisonment and immediately revert back to heterosexuality on gaining freedom.

Variational patterns attract many to homosexuality as a means of variety or to escape boredom. The person may seek a new kind of experience but he has no compulsion to do so, nor is he compulsively attracted to homosexuality.

The external behavior of all three types may be identical; the motivation, however, is quite different. The reparative or true homosexual's behavior is compulsive and necessary, while the other two types are neither.

To call a mere user of sexual relief by homosexual means a homosexual is erroneous and unjustified. Unfortunately our worse than useless sex laws (many of which are crimes against nature themselves rather than the sex acts they label as crimes) make no distinction between a male caught in a single homosexual act— it might even be his first—and the true homosexual who is exclusively or predominantly homosexual. Prosecuting and imprisoning him as a homosexual will effectively stigmatize him for life in the eyes of his friends and the public.

DO ALL HOMOSEXUALS ACT LIKE WOMEN?

Much of the public has the idea that all homosexuals are effeminate and act more like women than men. This conclusion is based on the fact that the only homosexuals they recognize are the mincing exhibitionists who show their contempt of society for its condemnation.

Most homosexuals are as masculine as most heterosexual men and are undetectable in a crowd. They have all of the characteristics of a male, with one exception—their sexual desires center on members of the same sex. Most of us have associated with them without even suspecting that they were homosexuals. They might be relatives, friends, or even our own children.

True homosexuals will shy away from the overt effeminate type. In the first place, they unconsciously fear women, and in the second place, they are reluctant to attract attention to themselves by making public displays of their homosexuality. If you were to ask one of them how he feels about the effeminate type, you would probably receive this reply. "If I wanted a woman, I'd get me a real one, not a make-believe one."

IS HOMOSEXUALITY A SIN?

For many centuries homosexuality has been vigorously condemned as a practice of wicked sinners doomed to eternal damnation. This should not be surprising, however, because false conceptions of the sex urge (resulting from ignorance of its true nature) have plagued Christianity since its birth. Sexual theories based on the erroneous belief that sex is an invention of the devil to be shunned at any cost have caused untold confusion, agony, and frustration. Instead of learning the biological facts of the human body, we still irrationally quote the Bible, which is not a textbook on biology.

Most of us base our dislike or even hatred of homosexuality on the Old Testament myth of the destruction of Sodom and Gomorrah. It is not the word of God but a myth made to emphasize a point, an invention of the Hebrew priests to frighten the people away from homosexuality so that they would use their sexual energies for the creation of children so as to increase their small population. The Hebrews, not God, made it a sin.

William Graham Cole, a noted authority on religion and sex, explains Sodom and Gomorrah as follows:

> The story in Genesis 19 is, in the minds of Old Testament scholars, clearly a mythological attempt to account for the destruction of a city which had once been located near the Dead Sea. The city's destruction by fire and brimstone indicated volcanic activity, but there was no volcano in the region of the Dead Sea, which suggests the story had been brought from another locale. If the myth had grown up in the valley, the agent of destruction doubtless would have been water and not fire, an inundation by the Dead Sea itself—a supposition supported by the fact that Genesis traces the origin of the sea to this event, the destruction of Sodom and Gomorrah.

The fact that water, not fire, destroyed the cities was verified by an archeological expedition of April 29, 1960, under the leadership of Dr. Ralph E. Baney, a Baptist missionary-explorer from Kansas City, Missouri, when he announced the discovery of Sodom and Gomorrah at the bottom of the Dead Sea. His discoveries indicated the cities were flooded when a protecting dike was ruptured by an earthquake.

Natural catastrophes have dotted the pages of history when man has been unfortunate enough to live where they occurred, as in the destruction of Herculaneum and Pompeii in A.D. 79, the result of the eruption of a volcano; in the death of 36,500 persons on Java and Sumatra in 1902, when the volcanic island of Krakatoa erupted; in the extinction of 40,000 persons resulting from the eruption of Mt. Pierre, Martinique; and in the death of 99,000 in the great Japanese earthquake of 1923, which destroyed Tokyo and Yokohama. Why not blame God for killing all these people because of their homosexuality?

The Hebrew priests, who also ruled, discouraged and condemned the use of all sex that did not result in children, because of their need for males for the army to protect them against their enemies and for females to till the soil.

Their motivation was not spiritual; they were seeking to preserve their independence. They simply disguised their objectives under a cloak of spirituality.

Frequently, quotations from Paul (Rom 1: 18-32) are used by ministers or priests to strike terror into the hearts of religious homosexuals, with the result that many of them leave the church because it is impossible for them to abandon their homosexuality. Some pastors, without the least regard for accuracy, make it appear as if the New Testament chapter mentioned above is concerned with homosexuality instead of idolaters. Upon examination, the title of the first chapter is Humanity Without Christ. It has two subdivisions; The Pagans Adore Idols, and Punishment of Idolaters. These headings do not give the slightest hint that it concerns homosexuality. In the contents, however Paul says:

> For while professing to be wise they become like fools, and they changed the glory of the incorruptible God for an image made like to corruptible man and to birds and fourfooted beasts, and creeping things. . . . For this cause [please note "for this cause"] God has given them up to shameful lusts: for their women have changed the natural use for that which is against nature, and likewise the men, having abandoned the natural use of women, have burned in their lusts toward one another . . . and as they have resolved against possessing the knowledge of God, God has given them to a reprobate sense so they do that which is not fitting, being filled with all iniquity, malice, immorality, avarice, wickedness; being full of envy, murder, contention, deceit, malignity; being whisperers, detractors, hateful to God, irreverent, proud, haughty, plotters of evil; disobedient to parents, foolish, desolate, without affection, without fidelity, without mercy . . .

St. Paul clearly did not have homosexuality as his target; he was aiming at idolaters who, because of their idolatry and because of their refusal to recognize God, left the use of women. The genuine homosexual never *leaves* the use of women because he never uses them. He does not have and never has had a desire for women. For all practical purposes he is allergic to women and is often repelled and nauseated at the thought of sexual intercourse with them. Unfortunately, neither Paul nor any of his contemporaries had the slightest idea of the psychological causes of homosexuality.

Without question, it is a grave injustice, senseless and utterly useless, to hurl distorted two-thousand-year-old quotations at homosexuals from the pulpit. There is no changing a physical and psychological condition that is unchangeable. The only possible result, in many cases, is to drive the already sensitive homosexual into irrational and abnormal guilt and fear, setting the stage for neurosis and even psychosis.

In spite of the fact that many ministers and priests condemn homosexuals, there are Christian authorities acquainted with the true nature of homosexuality who declare that homosexuality is not a sin. Father Marc Orison, an eminent French Roman Catholic writer who is both a doctor of theology and a doctor of medicine, has pointed out that, "logically speaking, the offense not being a mortal one, but rather a matter of weakness, there is no logical reason that a homosexual should go to confession after every lapse." He charitably looked upon homosexuals as human beings, not as dangerous monsters automatically doomed to eternal damnation.

From the psychological viewpoint, the Reverend H. Vandervelt and Dr. P. Odenwald, in their "Psychiatry and Catholicism," declare:

> Anxiety strongly influences the reason and the will . . . therefore, the moral responsibility for actions in an anxiety state is often so reduced that mortal sin is excluded, and in some cases there is no question at all.

Because true homosexuality develops from a state of fear and anxiety and because the homosexual is *incapable* of heterosexuality, there can be no question but that he is sinless unless he resorts to coercion or violence in his sexual practices.

God himself does not condemn the homosexual, as demonstrated most forcefully by Michelangelo, a homosexual who is considered to be the greatest sculptor of religious masterpieces in the history of the world. All the abilities any of us possesses come from God. Thus, not only did Michelangelo's artistic genius come from God but, he also must have been *inspired* by God when he conceived his great religious masterpieces. Here we have God Himself picking a homosexual as a recipient of special favors. Is it possible that human judgment is superior to divine judgment?

WHO ARE THE HOMOSEXUAL PERSECUTORS?

Many heterosexuals filled with sexual guilt and fears attempt to appease their guilty consciences for socially or religiously condemned activity by the psychological process known as "projection." In other words, they transfer their own guilt to the homosexual and vent their self-hatred in the form of humiliation, persecution, and hatred of the homosexual. Homosexuals thus become the whipping boys for heterosexuals who seek to escape from their own guilty consciences.

A second group of homosexual haters are suppressed homosexuals who fight off their own homosexual desires by persecuting those who feel free to do what they themselves long to do.

A third group is comprised of genuine homosexuals and those who use homosexual outlets when it suits them and who actually condemn others like themselves in self-defense against a brutal and intolerant society.

Don Thomas Moore, in his book *The Driving Forces of Human Nature,* describes the mental processes in the second and third groups in these words:

> Men not only want to think well of themselves but also to have the world esteem them highly. If, therefore, they have motives or desires that the crowd condemns, they defend themselves by disguising the workings of their minds. A common way of doing this is to manifest horror or disgust at the recital of

the deliquencies of others by what might be termed an old-maid shock reaction. A certain amount of regret at the unfortunate actions of others is natural, and its manifestation has no particular significance. When, however, anyone betrys extraordinary disgust and expresses himself in very strong terms about the matter, his shock reaction is a "complex indicator." He himself has a great deal of trouble with the matter he condemns. His manifest disturbance and horror about the affair is a defense reaction which keeps anyone from suspecting that one who is violently shocked would ever dream of such delinquencies.

Dangers of Sex Activity of Young with Adults Exaggerated

Nothing is so firmly believed as what we least know.

MICHEL DE MONTAIGNE

One of the most uncalled-for fears parents have is the false belief that homosexuality can be "caught" by their children, like measles, from homosexual contacts or seduction. Actually, most boys go through a homosexual period before they emerge as heterosexual adults in what seems to be a natural stage in their sexual development. The truth is that neither the homosexual nor the heterosexual unless he is mentally deficient or deranged, has any desire for immature and undeveloped sexual partners when he can easily find older and more experienced companions. Ordinary common sense should make this evident. In addition, most of them are intelligent enough to realize that children are unpredictable or may feel so guilty by the sexual experience that they may tell their parents or report such adults to the police. If the truth were known, many apprehended adults are actually seduced by children.

Men who are child molesters are not even in the same psychological category as homosexuals. They belong to an entirely different classification of sexual deviants and are known as pederasts. The reasons for their being have no similarity whatsoever to those causing homosexuality. Child molesters obviously are abnormal personalities who are extremely childlike and immature in the whole of their emotional life. To place homosexuals in the same category with child molesters is absurd.

The reason why they murder children is pointed out very clearly in Dr. Benjamin Morse's book *The Sexual Deviate*.

> Most commonly, the pederast kills to keep from being found out (not from a desire to kill). Once his sexual fury has abated, he realizes that he has done something which society strongly

condemns, and that he is faced with the possibility of a prison sentence. Punishment, in most cases, is but a secondary hazard. The fear of exposure, of public knowledge of the crimes, of the scorn of friends and relatives—this is what makes him a murderer.

When society has the common sense to demand—instead of fight against—sex education, it may come to the realization that its own violent reactions often are the direct cause of child murders. It will also learn that creating great fear in the pederast of the consequences of his act may cause him to kill in self-defense, for the purpose of destroying the chief evidence and witness against him. Without a doubt, society creates its own monstrous child slayers by its irrational fears and desire for revenge.

Public demand for the imprisonment of male homosexuals is based on the false belief that they constitute a grave menace to children. Donald J. West, author of *The Other Man,* says, "The great majority have no sexual interest whatsoever in children."

He points out that with youths of seventeen and eighteen, it is a different matter, for many homosexuals find them attractive in exactly the same manner that heterosexuals find girls of that age attractive. When the public comes to the realization that males reach their peak of sexual potency between the ages of sixteen and twenty and enjoy sex as much if not more than adults, they may cease their demands for punishment of adults caught, so to speak, en flagrante delicto with youths. At that age, most of them know perfectly well what form of sexual pleasure they desire, and they often take the initiative in homosexual advances. As a matter of fact, unscrupulous youths often exploit their ability to tempt older men, sometimes for financial gain, fully realizing that if they get caught, the *older* man is blamed by the police and public. This manifest injustice could be stopped by recognizing the fact that these youths are sexually mature persons whose sex drive is operating at full capacity.

The famous Wolfenden Report, probably the most extensive and authoritative document ever made on homosexual offenses and conducted at the request of the Moral Council of the Church of England for the British Parliament by a committee of fifteen talented and outstanding authorities, found that the seduction of children by homosexuals was a myth. The report stated:

> It is the view held widely, and one which found favor amongst our police and legal witnesses, that seduction of youth is a decisive factor in the production of homosexuality as a condition, and we are aware that this view has done much to alarm parents and teachers. We have found no convincing evidence to support this contention. Our medical witnesses unanimously held that seduction had little effect in inducing a settled pattern of homosexual behavior, and we have been given no grounds from other sources which contradict their judgment. Moreover, it has been suggested to us the fact of being seduced often does less harm to the victims than the publicity which attends the criminal proceedings against the offenders and the distress which undue alarm sometimes leads parents to show.
>
> We have, it is true, found that men charged with homosexual offenses frequently plead that they were seduced in their youth, but we think that plea is a rationalization or an excuse, and that the offender was predisposed to homosexuality before the seduction took place. We have little doubt that this account of the origin of their condition is so frequently given by homosexual offenders that it has led police and the courts to form the impression we have mentioned.

In addition to parents' unwarranted fear that homosexuality is communicable through sexual association with homosexuals is the at times hysterical belief that sexual association with adults is a mental, physical, and spiritual disaster that will ruin the child for life.

This has been proved to be just another of those false and unfounded opinions or beliefs that we entertain because of our appalling ignorance and our unnatural and twisted sexual attitudes. (Today many young persons, because of their hatred for the evident sexual hypocrisy of their elders, are rebelling against the idea of the evilness of sex.) Shocking as it may seem to many people, if children are either instructed or introduced to sex with gentleness and kindness, they will receive the impression that sex is something good and this awareness will lead them to a happy sex life. To have them wait until they are juniors and seniors in high school before offering them sex education is like locking the door after the horse has been stolen. By that time they will already have received so much misinformation and heard so many myths, falsehoods, and nonsense that it will be difficult to change the course of their sexual life. Their early impressions are all registered on their subconscious minds and could be erased only by a psychiatrist.

Several years ago two psychiatrists, Drs. Lauretta Bender and Alvin E. Grugette, Jr., of Bellevue Hospital, New York City, conducted an exhaustive study of several thousand adults who as children had had sexual experience with adults, either through seduction or molestation, and found, amazingly, that the experiences had not left any lasting bad effects. Could this be possible? Were not children who had had sexual encounters with adults ruined for life mentally, physically, and spiritually? The two psychiatrists made several startling discoveries.

These victims of molestation or participants in serious acts with adults had, with few exceptions, made normal adjustments in later life. The psychiatrists found that the ones who had not adjusted were headed for abnormality anyway, having shown symptoms before the experience of mental disease which may have contributed to their sexual activity.

They also discovered that many attractive children are the aggressors, using their charms to aid them in the role of the seducer. These children usually came from homes where they received little or no affection, or where there was an unnatural, fear-filled sexual atmosphere. We might ask: How many homes do have a natural, unaffected, healthy, happy sexual atmosphere?

Dr. Karl Menninger, who has the reputation of being one of the most brilliant psychiatrists in the world and a noted authority on human behavior, in his book *Love Against Hate* explains the psychological cause of parental disturbances over the sexual activity of their children as follows:

The horror with which most parents learn of their children's interest in various forms of sexual play is a reflection on the ambivalence in adult attitudes toward sexuality. Especially to their own children's sexuality. Freud pointed out that parents are actually jealous of their own children, that they try as long as possible to prevent them from any theoretical or practical acquaintance without sexuality, punishing them for premature excursions into this forbidden field.

In frank words, parents unconsciously feel the sexual pull toward their own children of the opposite sex and even—remember, *unconsciously*—desire sexual intercourse with them. This they dare not engage in because of the social ban on incest, consequently, they display jealousy. *Unconsciously* they resent anyone else doing what they cannot, and attempt to prevent any such occurrences. Sex is not mental but biological; it has no conscience. It can only be controlled by the mind and conscience of an individual properly trained to do so. Any mind filled with shame, guilt, and fear of his sexuality can never be trained to control sexual urges.

"It is an interesting corollary to this observation," continues Menninger, "that the sexual approach of adults to children is associated with the most intense feelings of social disapproval; such episodes have not infrequently served as a basis for mob violence against the offender." The assumption is, of course, that children are irreparably ruined by such experiences. Without intending in the least to justify or excuse such behavior, I may, nevertheless, point out that, in the cold light of scientific investigation, no such devastating effects usually follow. Let me repeat: no such devastating results usually follow. Two psychiatrists (Lauretta Bender and Abraham Blow) recently made a careful follow up of such cases and concluded that "children exposed to premature sexual relations with adults (this fact will seem unbelievable to those parents who believe their children would be irreparably damaged) frequently turn out to be unusually charming and attractive in their outward personalities."

How is this possible? Could it be that these children received, through a gentle and pleasing sexual experience, an indelible impression that sex was nothing to be ashamed of, nothing to feel guilty about and nothing to fear, thus freeing them from a life of shame, guilt, and fear which in turn would surely have ruined

what turned out to be unusually charming and attractive personalities?

> The conclusions [continues Menninger] drawn from such
> observations need not be shocking; they simply bear out our
> contention that sexuality is not the evil and horrible thing that it
> is generally conceived to be. Such experiences are traumatic
> [emotionally damaging] to the child only when connected with
> deep hostilities; the furtive and desperate nature of such attacks,
> combined with the attitude of society toward them, tends entirely
> in the direction of unbearably stimulating the child's hostilities
> so he conceives sex as brutality. But when the experience actually
> stimulates the child erotically, it would appear from the observa-
> tions of the authorities above mentioned that it may favor rather
> than inhibit the development of the social capabilities and mental
> health in the so-called victims.

Many of the uncivilized and savage tribes of Africa, the South
Sea Islands, and elsewhere in the world instinctively treat sex as a
natural function. They do not use the Christian method of shame,
guilt, fear, and punishment to force their simple rules for its control.

Rudolf Von Urban pointed out that, in some tribes of Africa,
adults taught masturbation to the children of the opposite sex because they believed it to be an important factor in sexual development. Amazingly, in contrast to children in the United States,
among these primitive children there were no reactions of repug-
nance, no depression, no sexual activity, no guilt feelings, no fear
of the sexual instincts, and no fear of their own bodies. The children of these un-Christianized, uncivilized savages were sexually
relaxed, happy, and healthy—undisturbed by emotional conflicts
brought on by unnatural and unrealistic sexual attitudes. Culti-
vation of a happy and healthy sex life for their children was to
these primitive people an important and sacred task—not something to be opposed and condemned because it might teach their
children immorality.

In Bronislaw Malinowski's classic, *The Sexual Life of Savages
in Northwestern Melanesia,* based on an extensive two-year study,
he describes the sexual life and customs he found.

These savages treated sex as a natural function of the body—as God would want them to—not as an invention of the devil to lure people into hell nor as an evil to be suppressed and kept secret. In this society, in direct contrast to that of the United States, with its numerous, basically sexual, social problems he found no sexual perversions; no functional psychosis; no psychoneurosis; no sex murders. There was, in the language, no word for theft. Homosexuality and masturbation were nothing other than imperfect means of achieving sexual gratification.

The amazing fact is that these uncivilized Trobrianders were much more sensible and realistic and thus much healthier sexually because they were not confused and bewildered by Christian sexual Bible quotations, unrealistic theories, and ideas now proven biologically false. Vast numbers of Americans who long ago deserted Christ's word and example concerning sexual sinners, nonetheless, under the cloak of the Christian religion, act like barbarians in their un-Christian abuse of homosexuals, illegitimate children, unmarried mothers, and prostitutes, and in their persecution of so-called immoral and criminal sexual activities. Even the pagan Trobrianders knew better.

The natural instincts are biological facts which can neither be effaced from the earth nor be basically altered. Like everything living, man needs first of all satisfaction of his hunger and gratification of his sexual instinct.

DR. THEODORE REIK

When and where did our present unnatural attitudes about sex originate? How did we become obsessed with our unnatural and unhealthy beliefs concerning its evils? What were the Hebrew beliefs concerning sex? Did Christ, the founder of Christianity, make sexual abstinence a keystone to his religion? How did the unnatural Hellenistic sexual dualism become part of Christianity, in spite of the fact that Christ was a sexual naturalist?

In order to understand our beliefs and attitudes it is necessary to examine the historical background of sex in the religious practices and theories of the Hellenistic Dualists and Hebrews.

The Hellenistic culture began in the fourth century before Christ, originating after Alexander the Great conquered Asia Minor, and was a mixture of Greek and Oriental. Cole terms the outlook of the Hellenistic culture "dualism" and that of the Hebrews as "naturalism." Interpretations of sex in the West have been either one or the other or sometimes, a combination of both.

Dualists believed the body was a prison from which the immortal soul had to be released. Their goal in life was to overcome the sordid demands of the body and obtain liberation of the spirit through spiritual contemplation. They believed that only by practicing asceticism and rigidly checking gluttony, greed, and—especially—lust would they be able to save their souls. They shrank from nudity, praised virginity and celibacy. They regarded sex as low and degraded, an act during which man descends to the level of a beast. Today you constantly hear people talking about our lower natures, condemning nudity, and expressing Hellenistic dualistic beliefs about sex, little realizing, although they profess to be Christians, that Christ was a Naturalist and had nothing to do with such theories.

Naturalism took a positive and accepting attitude toward the material and physical world, and the naturalist accepted the sex urge with gratitude and joy and as good and wholesome. Hebrew naturalism contrasts markedly with Greek dualism.

The Bible begins with the story of Creation, which naturally includes man's sexual nature. As the Scriptures say, "And God saw that it was good" and it observes that at the end of six days, "God saw everything that he had made, and behold, it was very good." There is nothing to indicate God looked on his handiwork and saw that everything was good except man's sexual organs and sexual nature. The Bible portrays God as commanding his creatures to be fruitful and multiply, nowhere does it even hint at celibacy or praise virginity. It is obvious that the Old Testament sees man as a creature created by God to enjoy the material world, including his body.

The early Hebrews enjoyed a high degree of sexual freedom and were not filled with guilt and fear over participation in it. Neither did they act as if the devil had been the creator of their sexual organs. In comparison with our present attitudes, they were lusty and free. True, adultery was sternly forbidden, but this arose from Jewish concern with the family line, not because the people were antisexual. The complete absence of any ban on fornication offers further proof of the lack of anti-sexual attitude.

However, the Hebrews did condemn homosexuality and onanism, which by some twisting at original meaning and misinterpretation became a condemnation of masturbation. Today we even use onanism as a term for masturbation. The origins of the Hebrews' prohibition of homosexuality has already been discussed in chapter 5.

The story of Onan, as found in the Old Testament is as follows: "Judah therefore said to Onan, his son: Go in unto thy brother's wife and marry her that thou mayest raise seed to thy brother. He, knowing that the children should not be his, went in unto his brother's wife, spilled his seed upon the ground, lest children be born in his brother's name. And therefore the Lord slew him because he did a detestable thing." (Gen. 38: 8-11)

Masturbation indeed. The definition of masturbation is the production of orgasm through manipulation by hand or other artificial stimulation of the sex organ.

There is no reference to artificial manipulation in this passage. The only words having any possible connection would be "spilled his seed upon the ground." Probably someone, sometime, desiring to condemn masturbation as a sexual activity, took the liberty of taking two disconnected passages and joining them together so it would appear that God condemned it. It could easily be managed, thus: Onan spilled his seed upon the ground and therefore the Lord slew him because he did a detestable thing, the "detestable thing" actually being Onan's refusal to father a child and consequently spill his seed upon the ground.

The story really tells us that Onan had sexual intercourse with his dead brother's wife and, at the moment of ejaculation, withdrew his penis, spilling his semen upon the ground. The cause of Onan's orgasm certainly could not be classed as artificial stimulation. It might be termed contraception by withdrawal—withdrawal is a common practice today to prevent pregnancy but it is never considered to be masturbation.

Some people still believe that the sin of Adam and Eve was the sex act. This represents a complete misunderstanding of the myth. None of the Jewish rabbis, nor any of the Christian theogians, interpreted the fall of man in sexual terms, but rather because of pride and rebellion against God. The church's negative attitude toward sex has misled many into the belief the fall of man was caused by sex.

In the Gospels of the New Testament, Jesus shows little concern about sex either by word or example. He never indicated the concern—you might even term it "obsession"—with sex that the Catholic Church still seems to indicate. Jesus was not interested so much in *what a man did but in what he was*. On the other hand, the Jews believed that all behaviour was a symptom of inward feelings; as a man thought within himself, so he was. Jesus looked for the motive behind the act and the meaning it had when the entire personality was considered; he was interested in the *inner motives* rather than the *outer acts* of men. The inner attitude of integrity, not the outer conformity to fixed standards, characterized all that Jesus said and did.

The Scribes and Pharisees judged men by their conformity to the Law; they believed that law governed all aspects of human behavior. But Jesus saw that the law dealt principally with human motives and attitudes. He penetrated into the motives of men and knew when they did right things for wrong motives. They never deceived him by righteous and pious activity for the purpose of social approval. If Christians were true followers of Jesus, the inner worth of a man would truly determine his worth, and conformity to the law would not determine his innocence or guilt. Psychologists or psychiatrists in our present civilization are the ones who could determine a man's motives.

Jesus emphasized the law of love (he never excluded sexual love) and made it the central theme of all of his teachings. All men were to regulate their lives through the love of God. He taught the revolutionary doctrine that God loves all men—saint and sinner alike—and because the sinner's need is greater, he holds the higher priority in God's concern for humans.

The pharisaic practice of and belief in rewarding the virtuous, punishing the wicked and rigidly separating the virtuous from all contaminating influences was repudiated by Christ's association with whores, sensualists, harlots, and other sinners. What happened to Christ's example? Just who among the so-called Christians are his followers? No wonder Chesterton said, "The Christian ideal has not been tried and found wanting; it has been found difficult and left untried." Many of us hate the Negro, persecute and jail the homosexual, think it is horrible if an unmarried girl becomes pregnant, despise illegitimate children, hate our own bodies because of their sex organs, condemn the naked body as if it were a creation of the devil, and do the very things that Christ repudiated by his own example.

Christ said he came to seek and save the lost, not to save the righteous but sinners in repentance. He said that harlots and publicans would get to heaven before the Pharisees. By his stories of the lost sheep, the prodigal son, and the lost coin, he emphasized that God's concern was for the lost. He emphasized too the love of God for his creatures, and taught that they were to love God and one another. In other words, that love is the law of life, the first and greatest of all the commandments. He certainly was never recorded as declaring that that "Thou shalt not commit adultery" and "thou shalt not covet thy neighbor's wife" were the greatest of all the commandments, as many Christians seem to believe, by their hatred of sex and public actions. You might even imagine that many of the pastors preaching from the pulpits of our churches were reincarnated Pharisees, judging from their sermons.

An outlook of therapy and redemption characterized all of Jesus' dealings with individuals. Unlike the Pharisees, he placed human welfare above the obstructions of the law, and found human need more necessary than ritual requirements. He sought the spirit instead of pressing for the letter of the law.

These principles were followed by Jesus in all of his actions and words, including those concerning sex and marriage. If sex is really the evil it is often pictured, to be guarded against and suppressed, why did not Jesus say so? He never so much as mentioned masturbation and homosexuality. If they were such terrible practices, why didn't he condemn them?

He did mention adultery in Matthew, saying, "You have heard that it is said, 'Thou shalt not commit adultery,' but I say to you that everyone who looks at a woman lustfully has already committed adultery within his heart." This does not make Jesus an ascetic, as he is frequently portrayed. This verse is often taken out of context in order to give it such an interpretation. In its correct setting, it is plainly an example of Jesus' emphasis on *intention or motive*. What he is saying is that there is no virtue in abstinence when one is filled with lustful desire.

Obviously Jesus regarded sex as wholesome and normal, in spite of those people who condemn it and yet pretend to be followers of Christ. The early Christians, in the verse above, misinterpreted Jesus completely when they determined it meant that all sexual impulses were evil. It was here that Hellenistic dualism regarding sex took over, replacing the naturalism of Jesus. Jesus never suggested that sex is evil in itself and so to be avoided or prohibited. It is only when sex becomes an idol to worship that it is a roadblock to salvation.

Jesus' concern, in the case of the adulteress, was not with her actions but with her attitudes. He understood and forgave and did judge her by the letter of the law. His action was one of desire to redeem and heal. He was not shocked at her sexual sin and did not indulge in self-righteous and legalistic denunciation. To him, it was a minor sin in comparison with the enormous spiritual pride of the Scribes and Pharisees.

When Jesus came upon the adulteress surrounded by men who asked him which of them should cast the first stone, he wrote in the sands the names of the women with whom they had committed adultery and told them that he without sin should cast the stone. They all crept guiltily away, and Jesus, showing his great compassion, asked, "Woman, where are they? Has no one condemned thee?" She answered, "No one, Lord." Then Jesus said, "Neither will I condemn thee. Go and sin no more."

Mary Magdalene, the notorious harlot and associate of Jesus, became an active force in the development of Christianity. She was privileged to be the first person to discover that Christ had risen from the tomb; she was the first to see Christ and hear his voice after the Resurrection—in other words, she had the honor of being the first witness to the miracle of the Resurrection. Why, of all people, should Jesus choose her, a harlot, to play such an outstanding role? Was it not because Christ desired to emphasize, by his example, God's mercy and compassion toward sexual sinners? Today, two thousand years later, many Christians exaggerate the gravity of sexual sins, enlarging them to enormous proportions, completely out of line in comparison with sins of far greater magnitude.

Society makes little allowance for motivation in sexual activity. All sex, according to the law, must be in marriage, even if the marriage is simply a legal permit to have sexual intercourse—in other words, merely a selfish relationship in which the partners exploit each other's bodies. The use of sex can be evil, but sex itself is never evil. It is evil when the motivation is evil—for example, when it is motivated by selfishness, viciousness, or desire for domination, or when it is obtained through the use of force. It is never evil when the motivation is good, as when the motivation is friendship, affection, and love.

Our present unnatural and confused sexual attitudes in the Western world began about A.D. 80, when the Christians developed the belief that intemperance and wantonness could be overcome and cured by asceticism—by rigorous self-denial or abstinence from sexual gratification. Christianity then departed from the naturalism of Christ and the Jews and allowed Hellenistic dualism in sex to invade its teachings. Instead of acting as Christians in sexual matters we soon became Hellenistic dualists.

The word "flesh" as used by Jesus, but more often by Paul, became a word of confusion. No one knew whether it meant the use of sex or flesh meat; the conflict was settled by a decision that Christians abstain from both.

Ascetism became a great problem for serious scholors during the first centuries of Christianity since the gospels had nothing in them that could be interpreted as a general command to practice sexual abstinence. Finally the supporters of abstinence pinned their doctrine on one single sentence of St. Paul: "It is good for man not to touch a woman," without the words or example of Jesus or anyone else to back it up. If this sentence was taken literally, Christianity would have committed suicide. It would have simply died out for want of members, since procreation would not have been possible without men touching women.

St. Paul was not a Hellenistic Dualist who regarded the body and its functions as evil; however, in matters of sex, he preached that celibacy was superior to marriage. Again we have a theory that is against the command of God to increase and multiply. Paul's advice was contrary to Hebrew naturalism and was almost purely Hellenistic.

The Church grew on the foundation Paul laid. With introduction of Hellenistic dualism in sex, sexual beliefs became a complex combination of Jewish naturalism and Hellenistic ascetism. Virginity became a cardinal virtue, and marriage a concession to the weak. Sex became an evil necessity of the human race, to be avoided and denied by the spiritually strong, and marriage thus became inferior to celibacy. Paul had unwittingly played an important part in guiding Christianity away from the Naturalistic teaching and example of Christ into Hellenistic-Oriental dualism in sex.

How could unmarried men be anything but chaste if they were forbidden intercourse with married or unmarried women? In those days all countries that allowed premarital intercourse prohibited intercourse with virgins and insisted on marital fidelity. The question was solved by prostitution. It was the safety valve for males when nature forced them to relieve their sexual tensions. Today the sex laws and social customs provide no legal safety valve before marriage.

Advocates of abstinence rejected prostitution as a solution to the sex problem. To add to the confusion, it was not long before it became quite obvious that asceticism was a complete failure. Since neither common sense nor logic could provide grounds for abstinence, its advocates invented astounding theories to support their claims.

For example, the philosopher Saturninus believed the world was full of angels and devils battling for the possession of men's souls. He advanced the ridiculous theory that evil spirits, led by Satan, had bestowed on man the sex urge which drove him to sexual intercourse and eventually into marriage and generation. According to this theory, Satan spawned the human race because he created the sex urge in man.

Christian theologians and philosophers actually debated for centuries the theory that because man was produced as a result of sexual intercourse, and since sexual intercourse was itself sinful because the sex urge had been bestowed on man by Satan, man himself was a sinful being.

St. Augustine, a disciple of Paul's, developed the theory of Saturninus into a sexual-moral theory of heredity, namely, the doctrine of original sin. Augustine looked on sex as highly dangerous and believed the best policy was total abstinence. (In his boyhood he was extremely promiscuous and evidently was sickened by sex. At the age of sixteen, it became so revolting to him that he turned to a belief in total abstinence.) He believed if one could not abstain, he should be sexually moderate within marriage, that sex should be preferably for procreation only, that mortifying the desires of the flesh was good for the soul, and that abstinence and virginity were pathways to God.

The Church resisted the Hellenistic belief identifying the body with evil and the soul with good, but in matters of sex, Hellenistic dualism became part of its teachings. Thus the teachings and example of Christ, the founder of Christiantiy, and his naturalism were abandoned in the struggle over the interpretation of sex.

Pope Gregory the Great (A.D. 590-604) adopted Augustine's doctrines, and declared that the lust of our parents' flesh was the cause of our being, so that even marital intercourse was consequently never free from sin.

Four factors can be cited as causing the conflicts and confusion in Christian morality today:

Society's abnormal and irrational concern with the prevention of procreation outside of marriage. (It causes irrational fears in parents and the mother, half a million illegal abortions, numerous suicides, and even murder of the newborn children).

The Christian beliefs as expressed in the Old Testament which are Naturalistic but condemn homosexuality and masturbation (using invented myths that have been discredited by our knowledge of today).

The words and example of Jesus, who was a complete Naturalist and condemned neither homosexuality nor masturbation.

Hellenistic dualism, which regards sex as evil and which Jesus never authorized nor preached.

Based on these Christian beliefs concerning human sexuality, the question of what is moral and immoral in sex has created the utmost agitation, turmoil, and confusion. Hellenistic dualism should be purged from Christianity because it is not a teaching of Christ and is the cause of the uneasy guilt and fear manifested in all sexual activity. Intellectually, it makes God out as a creator of evil. Emotionally, it is still the cause of the development of an immense amount of false guilt and irrational fear.

Ignorance is the greatest crime of all for it is a crime against the human mind.

ANCIENT PHILOSOPHER

Few of us realize the amazing lack of biological and psychological sexual knowledge of ministers, priests, and religious leaders. In 1958 (admittedly, some progress has been made since), Dr. Gelolo McHugh and J. Robert Moskin conducted a survey concerning the sexual knowledge and attitudes of Protestant ministers. (*Look,* magazine Nov. 25, 1958). Their findings showed that (1) a large percentage of Protestant ministers have practically no knowledge concerning the true functions of human sexuality, (2) much of the public's knowledge of sex comes from these pastors, so that we have a situation where the blind attempt to lead the blind, and (3) most of the counseling on sexual problems comes from these sexually uneducated ministers who, because of an appalling ignorance of this most vital of human functions are unprepared in viewpoint and training to give advice.

They reported the shocking discovery that, out of 228,000 ministers in America, only 15 percent could be called competent sex counselors. Thirty-five percent were aware that they should counsel but did nothing about it. Most appalling of all, 50 percent still preached that sex itself—let me repeat, sex itself—is evil; they actually believed that in discussing it, they would be teaching people how to sin. Can it be that we are still in the Dark Ages and don't know it?

It is dismaying indeed to think that one-half of all Protestant ministers in this country castigate God for creating man's nature as it is and as he meant it to be, but that is exactly what they do. One of the cardinal principles of Christianity is to accept God's will and have faith in him. How about accepting the question of the human body—sexual organs and all—as God created them?

It is another tragic truth that these same ministers, by their unnatural and ignorant conception of sex, poison the minds of their parishioners with the terrible evils of unnatural guilt, irrational fears, and destructive self-hatred and hatred for others that can, and frequently does, end in fearful violence.

McHugh and Moskin made these very intelligent suggestions to ministers.

1. They must rid themselves of their aversion to discussing sex. Only through education and the understanding that comes with knowledge can they free themselves from their ignorance and unconscious fear of sex.

2. They must learn to accept people as they are and as God created them instead of thinking of themselves (in their ministry) as God's infallible judges.

3. They must unlearn the church-taught lesson that sex is an animal or bestial function, part of man's "lower nature." (How can the source from which all love flows in man be part of his "lower nature?") Instead they should think of it as natural, as the most rewarding and beneficial of all types of human affection, and as a gift from God instead of an invention of the devil.

They also pointed out these vitally important sexual facts that ministers must learn to accept.

1. We are leaving children to find out about sex through the trial and error method.

2. We fail to teach children about sex before they develop the biological need for it.

3. Our social rules fail to recognize the realities of our sexual nature.

4. The mystery and hush-hush surrounding sex drives young people into marriage without the proper foundation to make them successful, thus opening the way to unnecessary divorces.

5. We open the doors to a tremendous number of marriages whose only purpose is to explore sex.

Individual ministers deal with sex according to their own home training. Since a large proportion of them come from religious homes where sex is considered evil, they are, consciously or unconsciously, sex haters who unconsciously pass on their hatred to their congregations, often with devastating psychological results.

When the problem of homosexuality comes up, most ministers are helpless. They simply have no psychological knowledge of its causes. Ninety percent of those questioned by McHugh had faced the problem but admitted they lacked the necessary knowledge to do anything about it. In a survey of Presbyterian pastors, he found that they ranked homosexuality as the problem they felt least able to deal with. Homosexuals, because of this lack of knowledge, might as well seek understanding and help from a blacksmith or a ditch digger.

Catholic priests are in even a worse position, having only their seminary training as a background for sexual counseling, which, unfortunately, has a negative angle, emphasizing its sinfulness. They too usually come from religious families believing that sex is an evil, often causing them to pass on their own feelings and so contaminate their congregations with unnatural guilt, irrational fear, and self-hatred. Since priests are not allowed to marry, they have no actual experience of marriage, and as St. Anselm observed, "Whoever does not believe will not experience, and whoever does not experience will not know. For, just as experiencing a thing far exceeds the mere hearing of it, so the knowledge of him who experiences is beyond the knowledge of him who hears."

Unfortunately, most priests not only have no experience but they also have little biological knowledge of the human sexual system or the psychological background to understand sexual problems. For this reason many can hardly qualify as sexual counselors.

Edward R. F. Sheehan, in an enlightening article on the Catholic Church in the *Saturday Evening Post,* entitled "Not Peace But the Sword" (Nov. 28, 1964, p. 41), points out a logical reason why many Catholic priests stress the wickedness of sex. "The practice of perpetual chastity," he writes, "can consume so much moral energy that the celibate ofttimes becomes arid, intolerant, and cold. Perhaps the reason so many priests seem to consider sexual purity the world's greatest problem is that it happens to be their greatest problem.

He also points out that there is, being heard among Catholic authorities, evidence that change will come because of a more realistic attitude by many priests concerning sexual matters. He quotes Father John Thomas, a prominent Jesuit sociologist, who believes the Church urgently needs to produce a whole new interpretation of sexuality. Father Thomas declares: "The most traditional moral formulations about sex are inadequate, both because they are culturally conditioned and because their proponents lacked adequate knowledge about sexual phenomena."

We get a very good idea of how sexual sins are emphasized in seminary training from Emmet McLaughlin, an ex-Catholic priest, in his book *The People's Padre*. He points out:

> A compendium of Roman Catholic moral theology, merely a summary of the several volumes studied in the seminary, devoted 32 pages of fine print to the infinitesimal detail of the multiplicity of sexual sins. In a mere 12 pages it disposes of the hierarchy's teachings on assault, murder, dueling, capital punishment, the relations among nations, and the morality of war from the Stone Age to the Atomic Age.

Why this seeming obsession with sex? Do the seminaries believe they can neutralize the sex drive by emphasizing its sinfulness? Do they believe sex is a function of the mind and can be erased by mental training? Do they not realize it is a biological function of the human body that can be regulated but not abolished by the mind?

Most Christian pastors, instead of learning and basing their teaching and counseling on the biological and psychological facts of human sexuality, use Bible quotations as their authority, and almost always from a negative approach. Unfortunately, the Bible, whose material comes from sources thousands of years old, is not a textbook of biology or psychology. It tells nothing of the biological or psychological reasons for the sexual functioning of the body. It tells nothing of the sex glands. It gives no information describing the filling of the sex glands and how they must be emptied when they become full. It gives no information about the nervous tensions created in the body by the pressure of full sex glands to a point where relief must be sought. It is utterly unreasonable to ignore the discoveries of the last half century in biology and psychology. Is it possible that the advancement of human progress and knowledge came to a halt two thousand years ago?

The Bible is not only valueless as a source of biology; it is the most misquoted, misinterpreted, and quoted-out-of-context book on earth. Not only that, it is probably the greatest source of confusion that exists in Christianity today in its present form. Even murderers and other criminals quote it to justify their crimes. Judges and lawyers frequently quote the Old Testament "eye for an eye, tooth for a tooth" aphorism as an excuse to sentence murderers to death, ignoring the words and example of Christ himself.

In the Bible you can find enough divergent quotations to seemingly justify slavery, witchburning, monarchy, and many other ills, too numerous to mention, which we today denounce as evils. The individual quoting from the Bible usually picks out—completely out of context, if it suits his purpose—the parts that make him feel the most comfortable with himself.

The Bible is a mixture of history and religious principles. Parts of it are mythical, exaggerated, distorted, and even false. The myths were used to demonstrate a point, and are not to be interpreted literally, as is so often done. Authentic historical accounts (if you can call historical accounts absolutely authentic because of the human element) and archeological discoveries have proven parts of the Bible to be exaggerated or untrue. History is not the word of God but the record of human events.

Unfortunately, those who accept it word for word never think of the fallibility of man. Even if God had dictated the Bible word for word two or three thousand years ago, it would, without doubt, have been altered extensively since then by human error, human misjudgment, human imagination, and human emotions. Since the writings of its various authors were gathered together and placed in one book by a council of the Catholic Church and named the Bible, it was copied by hand for centuries by individual monks who were reported to have changed words, paragraphs, and even the thought, according to their own individual viewpoint. To expect the complete Bible to be copied without error for many centuries is to credit human beings with having the perfection of God.

If human error in copying the Bible is not sufficient, just imagine translating it into hundreds of languages with their numerous differences in words and shades of meaning without error.

Other factors entering into the question of the accuracy of the Bible are human arrogance, human stupidity, and human pride. In the early period of the Christian Church written records were edited (how do we know what was deleted and what was added) and even destroyed in wholesale lots; consequently, many historical documents were distorted or lost forever. William F. Vassall, in his *The Origin of Christianity* points out: "The ancient Christians—Eusebius, Cyril, Theodosius, Augustine, Ambrosius, and others—boasted of the number of 'heretical' books they had destroyed." Using Lardner's *Gospel History* as his source, he adds: "Victor Tununensis, an African bishop, A.D. 566, said that while Messula was counsel at Constantinople in 506, by order of Emperor Anastasius, the Holy Gospels, having been written by illiterate evangelists, were censored and corrected." Only the good Lord knows what this censoring and correction did to the Bible.

If that is not sufficient, no one knows how many times the Bible has been rewritten, retranslated, deleted, or added to. History in it is sometimes distorted and false: some details are obviously garbled, incidents and events have gotten out of context, and prophecies are not always fulfilled. To believe literally every word in the Bible as the word of God is to attribute to him all the weaknesses of human beings. God is incapable of making the human errors which inevitably crept into the Bible for the simple reason he is God.

It seems as though it might be wise to reorganize the entire Bible to take out the inconsistensies, the noninterpretable portions, the history that is plainly not of a religious nature, the known errors, the myths that are constantly taken for facts, and the parts portraying God as a vindictive, vengeful, slaying God, whom any thinking person cannot possible reconcile as being one with the same God Jesus Christ described as the loving, gentle, and forgiving God of the New Testament—in fact, every part of it should be taken out that is not religious or connected with religion.

Cole states with much wisdom:

Until such a time as the church, clergy, and people take seriously once more the Gospel of Jesus Christ, reconciling the world, then the homosexual and the harlot, the adulterer and those caught in the perils and the problems of premarital relations will turn elsewhere, for . . . the church, after all, is not a club for saints; it is a hospital for sick souls, and all those who are sick in any way should find there the healing they so desperately need.

In the past ignorance of the true nature of sex by ministers and priests was excusable because none of us knew the true biological and psychological facts of human sexuality. However, today, when a large number of books,—even low-priced paperbacks—are available with the latest knowledge, there is little excuse, especially for those who do most of the counseling on sexual problems. Since all of our sexual laws and regulations can be traced back to religion, pastors have the moral obligation and solemn duty to become fully acquainted with the latest facts so they can fulfill their obligations as sex counselors. To obstinately cling to a few negative quotations from the Bible and neglect to acquaint themselves with the latest sexual knowledge is to allow themselves to remain a menace to the mental and physical health of their parishioners. Anyone who instills abnormal guilt and irrational fear and hatred of a natural function of the human body can be nothing less than a menace.

Fortunately, many Catholic and Protestant leaders are beginning to realize there is something fundamentally wrong with Christianity's attitudes and religious regulations concerning sex. The Catholic Church would do well to recall its embarrassment when it forced Galileo to deny his discovery that the earth revolves around the sun instead of the sun around the earth. Many Church officials, because of a fear of losing face, refuse to recognize the truth and change old teachings that science has proved false. Today, proved scientific facts concerning the sex urge can no more be denied than Galileo's discovery that the earth revolves around the sun.

Many Sex Laws—an Unconstitutional Invasion of Privacy

People crushed by law have no hope but by power. If laws are their enemies, they will be enemies to laws; and those who have much to hope and nothing to lose will always be dangerous more or less.

EDMUND BURKE

Most of our antiquated sex laws are useless and unenforceable, and consequently are themselves a major cause for the encouragement and increase of crime. They ignore the basic Anglo-American concepts of individual liberty and individual privacy, and fail to recognize the individual as an autonomous entity.

Sexual morality has never been successfully enforced by law and never will be. Sexual activity in private, with a few exceptions, should not be a legal problem but a problem of the individuals' own consciences.

For the law to decide what two consenting individuals should do sexually, in private, to satisfy their biological needs, verges on the incredible, if you pause to think about it. These laws actually infringe on the constitutional right of privacy.

Years ago, the Eighteenth Amendment failed miserably as an attempt to legally regulate the private drinking habits of Americans. It not only proved impossible to enforce but led to an immense increase in crime and disrespect for the laws of the country. It was a disastrous demonstration of futility. Fortunately, we had the wisdom to repeal it. The important question today is: Why repeal the law against the use of liquor (something that most people can use or not, as they choose) and still keep on the books laws against a human biological drive that is rooted deep in nature? Prohibition failed, and most sex laws are an appalling failure, proving that no law is stronger than the people's willingness to obey it and that morality is never obtained by law.

Why are the sex laws such an enormous failure? The answer

is simple. The sex drive is so powerful that there is no possible way to stop it short of death. It would be just as reasonable to pass a law reversing the direction of the earth around the sun. Man usually has the brains not to pass laws that conflict with the laws of nature, or, in other words, with the natural laws of God. Our sexual nature was planned by God and created by God and will never be effaced from the earth until God so wills.

Unquestionably, one of the prime factors in the failure of our sex laws is that legislators have never had the wisdom to distinguish between the *mere offender* against sexual customs and the *genuine* sex criminal.

It has been suggested by many enlightened authorities that all sex laws should be repealed except for:

1. Laws against violence, the use of force, and intimidation,
2. Laws to protect children, and
3. Laws to prevent actions that are a public nuisance. Morris L. Ernst, a distinguished lawyer, in a speech to the American Association for the Advancement of Science, pointed out:

> Our laws have attempted to abolish all sexual outlets except marital intercourse, nocturnal emissions, and, to some extent, solitary masturbation. The first Kinsey report says that 85 percent of all young males interviewed are criminals—since they make use of other sexual outlets. Remember that the difference between criminal and convict lies only in the fact of getting caught.

Judge Morris Ploscowe, author of the "Kefauver Committee Report on Crime in the United States," said:

> Granting that a state must continue to prohibit rape, protect children from sexual assaults and debauchery, and control prostitution, there still remain large areas of sexual activity which are presently prohibited by law and which may well be left to the domain of religion morals and esthetic. . . .

> Many of our sex laws are obsolete and almost completely ineffectual. They attempt the impossible. They fail to distinguish between the commonplace and dangerous in sexual behavior; frequently, they punish both with equal severity. They lump together sex activity and psychiatric aberration.

Dr. Paul H. Geghart's opinion, after twenty-five years of research, is expressed in the 1965 "Kinsey Report on Sex Offenders." He says:

> My personal opinion is that the sex laws should be rewritten so that any act between two mature people—as long as it is engaged in voluntarily and in private—would be legal. [This is also the recommendation of the Anglican Church, the American Law Institute and Britain's Wolfenden Committee, and it is of the new sexual statutes adopted by the state of Illinois in 1961.] Such a law would be far more suited to our modern world—and would result in fewer injustices—than old-fashioned statutes now on the books.

Regarding "mature people," he points out:

> It is difficult to draw an arbitrary line to establish sexual maturity at any point; but if a line must be drawn, we believe that there are many reasons for thinking it should be set at sixteen. The average sixteen-year-old girl is biologically an adult; she is sexually mature, has developed all the physical strength and coordination required for living in our society, and has at least a basic knowledge of the kind of behavior that society expects. Until this century, in which childhood has been prolonged by a vast expansion of high school and college education, sixteen-year-olds were accepted as members of adult society, and many girls married at sixteen.
>
> Our feeling at the institute is that society makes a serious mistake in adopting laws and attitudes that set teenagers apart from the adult world. When we treat teen-agers like children, we encourage them to act like children, while in fact they are capable of acting like adults—if we will only let them.

It has already been mentioned that the male is at the peak of his sexual strength and activity between the ages of sixteen and twenty, usually several years before he gets married. Any law that attempts to block his sex urge without providing for some type of sexual relief is bound to fail.

Dr. Kinsey made many of us aware of the impossibility of enforcing our sex laws when he discovered that if they were enforced as any law should be enforced, 95 percent of all men would be in prison, convicted of sex crimes, and only 5 percent would be left to act as jailers—if you could imagine such a ridiculous situation.

Legislators have in the past produced sex legislation using such terms as "crimes against nature," "unnatural sex acts," "lewd and lascivious acts," etc. Today these same acts have been discovered to be as natural as sexual intercourse between male and female. Biologically, human beings have erogenous zones—in other words, zones with a concentration of sexually sensitive nerve endings provided by nature for sexual use. They consist, as mentioned earlier, of the mouth, tongue, lips, anus, breasts, and the genitalia, astounding as this wide range may seem to those people who believe the use of some of these biologically conditioned zones for sexual purposes is "unnatural" and a "crime against nature." In fact they are not even deviations. Crimes against nature or not, it has been estimated that half of all married couples engage in oral intercourse.

Wallace de Ortega, in his book *Man Is a Sexual Being* comments:

> "Crimes against nature" is, to say the least, an ambiguous term. If nature in general is meant, I am sure she has never been consulted in the matter. If the nature of the individual performer is meant, the acts are part of the individual's nature and hence cannot be perverse, unnatural, nor abnormal. . . .
>
> The chief problem that exists in sexual matters is whether the judgments and evaluations, with respect to any single act, are made by a scientific or a religious authority. This brings forward the matter as to normal and abnormal acts. Biologically, the human animal is acting within character by engaging in many kinds of acts that certain religionists would term sinful. The sinfulness of the acts is called abnormal, which of course is quite untrue. Pushed further for better clarification, most religious authorities would call the questionable act violations of nature or unnatural acts, which are equally incorrect.

There are three leading types of human sexual gratification. In the order of use they are masturbation, heterosexuality, and homosexuality. Antihomosexual laws are just as unenforceable and ineffective as those that attempt to prevent other types of sex. Judges often sentence homosexuals "to make an example" of them to deter others. The public and judges have a false conception of the effectiveness of "examples." How are you going to deter 30 million men who, it has been estimated, practice homosexuality by the "example" set by the conviction of a half a dozen. Laws are not passed to punish "examples"; they are presumably passed to catch and punish all offenders.

Judge Learned Hand, one of America's great jurists, said, "Criminal law which is not enforced practically is much worse than if it were not on the books at all. I think homosexuality is a matter of morals, a matter very largely of taste, and is not a matter that people should be put in prison about."

Dr. Robbins comments, There are multiple causes and multiple degrees and intensities of homosexuality. To me, this is one of the reasons why most of our laws are quite stupid. They simply do not make sense because they cut much too wide, and since society condemns homosexuality, the homosexual is apt to be easily victimized and blackmailed. The private life of two male adults should be their own business, and the law of the land, in my opinion, should so state."

Dr. Berg comments that the law should be concerned with safeguarding the liberty of the individual, regardless of whether he is homosexual or heterosexual, and whether his liberty is infringed upon by threats, blackmail, robbery, unwarranted interference, or assault. Since the law makes homosexuality a crime homosexuals are sitting ducks for all unlawful acts described above. He says, "If the law is going to act other than according to these principles, it is exercising an unwarranted interference with the liberty of the individual, and therefore no doubt is quite justly regarded by many of its victims as the criminal."

There is no other country on earth that has been so appallingly intolerant of homosexuals. In most other nations of the world homosexuals are accepted as human beings and not regarded as freaks. Great Britain recently made homosexuality legal. In Denmark, Sweden, and Spain, homosexuality between consenting partners is not punishable unless it involves the young or is an affront to public decency. In Belgium also it is only punishable if it is an affront to public decency. In France it is permissible by law for consenting partners over twenty-one. In Norway it is punishable only if enforcement is essential to the public interest. In Italy, Holland, and North Africa it is permissible, and in many parts of the mideast and East, where sex is regarded as a pleasant pastime (not as an invention of the devil), homosexuality is merely treated as an additional sexual outlet.

Many of our sex laws are presently being questioned on constitutional grounds because they (1) infringe on the First Amendment, providing for the separation of church and state, (2) infringe on the Ninth Amendment, guaranteeing the right of privacy; (3) in the case of homosexuals and the inmates of our prisons, infringe on the Eighth Amendment, forbidding cruel and unusual punishment; and (4) in the case of homosexuals, infringe on the Fourteenth Amendment, forbidding the denial of equal protection of the laws.

The First Amendment provides for complete separation of church and state. Since the release of sexual tensions is a biological necessity, sex cannot harm or damage anyone if acts are performed in private between willing partners. It could, however, in certain circumstances be considered a sin, but still in no way affect the public welfare; (consequently, it is quite ridiculous for the state to take over what are obviously the duties of the church. Sin, if it does not concern the public welfare, is the concern of religion and religion alone. The state has its hands full taking care of its own affairs, therefore the Supreme Court should declare all sex laws that infringe on the First Amendment unconstitutional.)

Religion is historically responsible for the state's intrusion into the realm of sin; consequently, religion should have the courage to use its influence to restore to the individual his freedom of choice in private morality. There can be no question but that his actions in his private sex life are the individual's own personal and private responsibility, therefore he should be allowed to make his own decisions regarding them without the threat and the fear of arrest and imprisonment.

The Ninth Amendment guarantees the right of privacy, a right that none of us wants invaded. Bennett B. Patterson's recent book,

Forgotten Ninth Amendment has convinced many authorities with its impressive arguments that there are fundamental rights of individuals rooted in the natural laws that are inherent, even though not enumerated, in the Bill of Rights. He asserts the Ninth Amendment recognizes these rights, one of which is the right of privacy, including the right to privacy in sexual matters.

In the United States there is an ungodly amount of malignant gossip about other people's private sex lives. Whenever this occurs it means there is something fundamentally evil with society. There is no excuse for people to demand the state, with its police powers, punish people for the way they handle their private sex lives. Why anyone should be so concerned with his neighbors' private life which does not concern the public welfare and does not affect him personally, is beyond understanding. No one forces anyone to use any sexual method that he does not approve of.

Not only do unenforceable sex laws encourage damaging gossip but they also subject people to the terrible crime of blackmail, a crime of far greater seriousness than any sexual activity that takes place between willing partners in private. The mere fact that these laws are on the statute books is sufficient to encourage the blackmailer to carry out his nefarious operations. Homosexuals especially are easy victims for blackmailers because of their fear of public discovery, and antihomosexual laws by their very nature help rather than hinder the blackmailer. In fact, anyone, even the heterosexual, can become a blackmail victim.

The constitutional right of privacy should guarantee all people their biological birthright to use their sex organs in private, in any way that suits them. Their sex organs belong to them—not to the state, not to the police, and certainly not to gossiping neighbors. As long as the sexual actions of people are harmless to others and do not affect the public welfare, the state has no right to interfere. Why squander time and money on the impossible task of preventing human beings from being human beings?

The Eighth Amendment forbids the use of cruel and unusual punishment. It certainly is cruel and unusual punishment to arrest and imprison homosexuals for using the only method of sexual expression they are psychologically suited for. To attempt to force a true homosexual to stop his homosexual activity would be similar to attempting to force him by law to stop eating, or sleeping, or urinating, and to expect him to satisy his biological sexual demands with the opposite sex would be very much like passing a law forcing people who fear snakes to eat rattlesnake meat.

In the case of prison inmates, the demoralizing problem of sexual starvation faces them. Unfortunately, no one has invented a way for prisoners to detach and deposit their sex organs for storage on entering the prison gates, to be reclaimed as they file out at the completion of their sentences. They have only one demoralizing choice—total abstinence or homosexual relations, with only one possible result—forced homosexuality. It is a known fact that heterosexual men often turn to homosexuality when it suits their fancy or when heterosexual outlets are unavailable. When a person is starving, he will eat tainted food rather than starve, and likewise when women are unavailable, heterosexuals do not worry a great deal about taking part in so-called unnatural and abnormal sex, since it is better than sexual starvation.

One of America's great penologists, Dr. Henry E. Barnes, said: "If one were consciously to plan an institution perfectly designed to promote degeneracy [homosexuality] he would create the modern prison."

Sexual starvation of imprisoned men imposes physical, mental, and emotional torture of the most appalling intensity. It definitely is a disgrace to Christianity and resembles in no way the mark of a civilized and intelligent people. The revenge-minded public may some day come to realize that sex without an outlet is like a steam boiler without a safety valve—when pressure builds up, it explodes, with disastrous consequences.

In prisons, when sexual pressures build up beyond control, the results are violent prison riots during which sexual orgies occur and prisons can be partially destroyed. Prison officials have stated that 95 percent of prison riots occur because of sexual starvation.

Joseph F. Fishman, the former Federal Inspector of Prisons, exposed all the horrors of sexual starvation in his startling and shocking book *Sex in Prison*. He points out:

Far more than half of the prisoners sent to penal institutions are at a time of their most intense virility, when the overwhelming tides of sex beat upon them with irresistible force. . . . Even those outside who give some thought to the plight of sexually denied young men can have no real idea of the physical, emotional, and mental torture which these young men go through during the period of confinement.

There can be no possible doubt that it is cruel and unusual punishment to deprive any human being of his sexual birthright. No man has a right to deprive any human being of his freedom to biological expression or his human right to function in the manner God designed and created him to function—as a sexual being.

Imprisoning homosexuals in a men's prison to either punish or reform them is incredibly stupid. How can you reform them—change them to heterosexuality—when there are no women and only men available? Can you imagine sentencing a male rapist to a women's prison, or an alcoholic to a brewery, or a drug addict to a drug-manufacturing plant? Certainly not!

The Fourteenth Amendment specifies that no state shall deny any citizen within its jurisdiction the equal protection of its laws, and yet we have a large number of homosexuals who are blackmailed, beaten, assaulted, robbed, and even murdered, and they are helpless because they do not have equal protection of the law.

Anti-homosexual laws by their very nature place all homosexuals in the intolerable position of being easy prey to vicious criminals who assault, rob, and blackmail them with impunity because the homosexual dares not report the criminal acts against him to the police. It is very simple. The criminal entices the homosexual into sexual advances, or even make the advances himself. He feels free to rob or blackmail the homosexual because he knows that, according to the law, the homosexual has committed a criminal act and dares not report the crime against him. Thus the true criminal uses the antihomosexual laws as a protective cloak for his crimes. If homosexuality were made legal, this would not be possible.

From a sexual standpoint practically every sexually mature

male in the United States is actually an enemy of the law, because 95 percent of them have broken the sex laws, many of them not just once or twice but hundreds of times. If it were possible to obtain an actual count of the number of sex crimes committed each year it would probably mount into the billions. Yet paradoxically, we are appalled and bewildered by the lack of respect for and obedience to our laws. Lack of respect for and disobedience of just one unenforceable law breeds disrespect for all laws.

There can be no doubt the sex laws are one of the great causes of American lawlessness and the increase of crime. Human beings, inherently, either consciously or unconsciously realize they can get by with breaking most of the sex laws without getting caught. This encourages them to further attempts to defy other laws; consequently, the nonenforcement of the sex laws has snowballed into a mass contempt and defiance of all laws.

If laws are neither sensible nor reasonable they will not be obeyed. Most sex laws are neither, for they attempt the impossible by seeking to override natural laws with man-made laws. If there is no public will to observe them, they are meaningless, and public will can exist only when the law is realistic and justifiable. There are not enough jails nor enough policemen nor enough courts to enforce any sex laws because *they are not supported by the people.*

All state laws should be repealed or rewritten to bring them into conformity with the natural laws and with the biological and psychological discoveries of the last fifty years. Unfortunately, it may take years and years to do this, state by state. A timesaving and less expensive method would be to submit them to the Supreme Court to test their constitutionality. There is no question but that most of them are unconstitutional for the simple reasons that they are unworkable, unrealistic, unobserved by 95 percent of the sexually mature; they are excessively severe, reveal an ignorance of human behavior; they are in conflict with the natural laws of human sexuality; and they encourage disrespect and disobedience of all laws and, consequently, increase and encourage criminality.

There are none so blind as those that won't see.

MATHEN HENRY

Unquestionably, the elimination of sexual fears and all their enormously damaging effects would in time eliminate a large percentage of the social plagues now rooted in these fears. The tremendous power of love freed from the chains of sexual guilt and sexual fears could and would work miracles for the happiness and peace of mind of man. If we could but realize the devastating effects of fear—and do something about them,—we could free the world of almost all hatred. It is startling but true that 90 percent of hatred is based on fear—much of it sexual fear; therefore, the first and greatest problem facing man is fear.

Most sexual fears are unreasonable fears. There is not the slightest doubt that man is basically a sexual being, and that sex is the hub around which his life revolves. His mental and physical health and his happiness depend on a life free from sex guilt and fear. His body, as God created it, is proof of his sexuality. His complete nervous system in one single network of nerves, all re sponsive to sexual stimulation at any of the erogenous zones—the special concentrations of sexually sensitive nerves in erogenous zones, the sex organs, anus, breasts, mouth, tongue, lips—even the earlobes. In some individuals, stimulation of any part of the body can produce an orgasm. Whether religion or the law agrees or not, what God has decreed is indisputable.

Man, because of his self-preservation drive, is so constituted that he always fears the strange or unknown. Until he uses the brains and intelligence God gave him and acquires the sexual knowledge to overcome his sexual ignorance, he will continue being filled with sexual fears. Only through knowledge will he gain sexual understanding and tolerance of his sexual nature.

Most Americans, no matter how much they enjoy sex or say

111

they do, have a hidden or unconscious fear of sexual activity and, consequently, an unconscious hatred of their sexual natures. As a result, simply because we have never been taught to accept our sexuality as God Himself created it, we are a nation of sex haters.

The appalling fact is that religious beliefs and our sexual laws have indelibly impressed on our minds the fact that there is no positive or good side to sex, there is only an evil or sinful or criminal side. As a result, we have been forced into sexual attitudes and beliefs that are unnatural, irrational, and abnormal. Few persons can escape the psychological impact of this negative approach without acquiring some unconscious guilts and fears, and hatred of the sexual nature.

Religion, because of a lack of knowledge of the biological construction of the human body, has in the past based its beliefs on theories and deductions that clash with the biological and psychological discoveries of recent times. The human body can function properly only according to natural law—not according to biblical quotation. Only when God and the natural law become identical will science and religion become reconciled. Natural law is God's infallible will, no matter what the beliefs of fallible man may be. In other words, man can be mistaken and often is. God can never be.

Christianity, especially, has, because of its disastrous obsession with the evils of sex, sought to suppress, check, and even smother the very function provided by God to balance and neutralize the aggression and violence of man's self-preservation instincts. It has created evils where no evils existed. It has filled the mind of Christians with the demons of false shame, false guilt, false fears, self-condemnation, self-hatred, and all of the inevitable consequences of frustration, anxiety, and nervous tensions. The result has been a fearful harvest of millions upon millions of unhappy, disrupted, distorted and broken lives filled with guilt, fear, and hatred, and ending in mental and physical diseases.

Without the least exaggeration, it can be said that an unnatural and irrational fear of sex is one of the horrors of Christian civilization. Countless human beings are senselessly, needlessly, and brutally being crucified on the cross of sexual fears—a crucifixion inspired and perpetrated by religion's negative approach and its ignorance of the biological and psychological aspects of human sexuality. Attempting to obstruct and counteract natural instincts will inevitably create human agony and suffering. Ignoring or refusing to follow natural laws of sexuality will automatically cause man to punish himself for his disobedience. God does not have to lift a finger.

Reik expresses this truth in forcible language.

> The fact that man is the only species which does not fulfill the natural laws of sexuality is the immediate cause of a series of devastating disasters. The external negation of life results in mass death, in the form of wars, as well as in psychic and somatic disturbances of vital functioning.

Hiding our heads in the sands of sexual superstition, sexual ignorance, and sexual intolerance is a negation of God's will. He gave us brains and intelligence and the power to reason for the most cogent motive—for us to use them. If we refuse to take advantage of these powers we can never attain a solution of the numerous social problems rooted in sex.

Few of us have the sexual knowledge to be aware of the amazing list of social problems that are rooted in human misunderstanding and ignorance. How many of us know that perceptive judges and lawyers report that probably 95 percent of all divorces have sexual incompatibility, sexual fears, sexual conflicts, sexual anxieties, or sexual frustration as the basic cause? How many of us realize that much of the violence that threatens us on the streets is rooted in the anger caused by frustration resulting from the denial of sexual gratification? How many of us know that alcoholism is acknowledged by some perceptive authorities to have it roots in sexual fears, sexual anxieties, or sexual frustration? How many of us even suspect that 95 percent of our prison inmates are there because of unresolved sexual conflicts? How many of us know that 95 percent of all crime is rooted in unresolved sexual problems? Do we realize that 95 percent of all murders are caused by sexual conflicts? Do we know that drug addiction is rooted in sexual problems? Do we know that a large percentage of suicides are caused by sexual frustration and sexual fears? Are we aware that homosexuals—true homosexuals —are to a large extent developed in a home atmosphere of sexual fears and maladjustment? Are we aware that sexual perversion—true perversion—develops from sexual fears? Do we realize that the reason for much of juvenile delinquency has a sexual basis? Do we accept the fact that a large percentage of the 60,000 cases of violent child abuse may be the result of parents' subconsciously believing the child is a product of sinful and wicked sexual actions? Do we know that all neuroses are caused by improper and insufficient relief of sexual tensions? Have we any idea that tension-caused diseases may be the result of sexual tensions stemming from sexual frustration, anxiety, guilt, and fears? But most of us know that these problems are blamed on almost every cause except sexual maladjustment.

Ministers, priests, religious leaders, and lawmakers can hardly have a desire to inflict such disastrous plagues on the population; nevertheless, that is exactly what they are doing because of their ignorance of the biology and psychology of human sexuality.

If we truly desire to face the realities of our sexual nature and eliminate the above social problems, which are really major calamities, we will discard our superstitions and illusions, forget the myths, and free ourselves from our unnatural and irrational sexual guilt and fears over its God-intended use. Then, and only then, can we neutralize and balance our aggressive instincts with sexual love. Guilt and fear and punishment for the natural use of our God-given sexual birthright will inevitably bring forth the aggression, violence, and hatred inherent in our self-preservation drive.

Anyone, if he stops to reason, will realize that, if God had created human sexuality for *limited use,* He would have created the body such that it could *only be used* in a limited manner. If he had created sex for procreation only, as in the animal world, humans would instinctively mate in the manner of animals. God is no trickster who cunningly created sex as a device for the downfall of men. He created sexual love to be used as the source of human love. He created the erogenous zones to be used—not to be declared out of bounds by ignorant men. It is beyond reason to imagine He created any part of the body that He did not intend to be used. In His Divine wisdom He anticipated man's sexual ignorance and foresaw man's attempt to all but abolish its natural functioning; consequently, He provided numerous biological safeguards to ensure its constant use. To demand abstinence from any form of sexual relief, from the time sexual maturity is reached especially in the male—the natural aggressor in sexual relationships —is a biological absurdity. There should be no question about the need for a common-sense, natural, and realistic control of sex based on present-day biological and psychological knowledge.

What we do not seem to realize is that most of the evils of sex —murder, sadism, rape, sexual assaults, bizarre and fantastic sexual perversion, violence in sexual relations, to name a few—are a direct result of our appalling sexual ignorance. Sensible, natural, and realistic sexual education could to a large extent eliminate true sexual evils.

Since religion has been creating sexual guilt and sexual fears for centuries, mainly because of ignorance of the biological make-up of the human body, it should, as a matter of common sense, wisdom and intellectual honesty, adopt a completely new and realistic code of sexual morality in conformity with the natural laws of human sexuality as God created it and the biological and psychological facts as we know them today.

Ministers and priests, since they are the ones most people consult on sexual problems, should be required to learn *in the seminary,* the fundamental biological and psychological principles of sex. That way, for most of the clergy, it will not be a matter of the blind attempting to lead the blind, as it is today.

Most sex instruction should be given in the positive, not the negative. We have been taught the evils of sex—in other words, the negative side—for so long that many of us do not even know there is a positive side to sex. For many of us our education has come through diatribes against sexual transgressions from the pulpit.

It should be the duty of parents to teach their young children about sex during their early years. Many parents know nothing more than how to perform the sex act, and here again it is a case of the blind attempting to lead the blind. It is, of course, impossible to do the impossible. Human sexuality covers a far broader field than sexual intercourse. Most parents simply do not have the sexual knowledge necessary.

Sex education must start somewhere, and the only place, at present, is in school. Because there are few teachers adequately knowledgeable in the field of sex education, the best qualified will have to be used. Eventually, colleges and universities should give courses and degrees in sexology in order to provide qualified teachers. Sensible, realistic programs will eventually be worked out, based on biological and psychological principles.

If we truly desire to free ourselves of the tragic social problems rooted in false sexual shame, false sexual guilt, irrational sexual fears, and the hate and violence generated by these psychological damaging emotions, and develop a natural, realistic, and healthy attitude toward our God-given sexual nature, it will be necessary for us to overcome our unnecessary guilt over and fear of our sexuality. Three essential steps will be necessary to accomplish anything toward that end.

1. Religion (being responsible for many of our sexual fears because of Christianity's centuries-old obsession that sex itself is evil) is bound in conscience, as a matter of charity and justice, to adopt sexual beliefs that recognize the biological construction of the human body as God created it. In other words, religion must alter its almost completely negative approach, and its acknowledgement of recently discovered biological and psychological sexual facts, and openly recognize the natural laws of human sexuality. Every effort should be made to free our sex-obsessed society from its unnatural concern with sex, its psychologically damaging sexual attitudes, and its unnatural and unrealistic fears of sex. One way is through positive instruction from the pulpits of our churches by pastors educated in sexology. Religious leaders, as a matter of conscience, are bound to use their God-given reasoning powers and intelligence for learning and disseminating the true facts concerning human sexuality, as known today, and to abandon the myths, superstitions, and false beliefs of ancient religious leaders who obviously had little knowledge of the anatomical makeup of

man and his physical and sexual functioning.

2. All penal laws that prohibit sex activity between consenting partners, carried out in private and without infringing on the rights of others or disturbing the public welfare, should be repealed. However, since the states show little interest in repealing them and since many authorities believe they are unconstitutional, the United States Supreme Court should rule on their constitutionality at the earliest possible time. They obviously menace the mental and physical health of the nation because they create an atmosphere of uneasy suspense, guilt and fear of sex in almost anyone, for no one knows even though the laws are seldom enforced, when he will be the victim of arrest and prosecution for breaking them. The laws are unnatural because they do not recognize the realities of the human physical makeup, therefore, they are contrary to the natural laws of human sexuality. They are unenforced, unenforceable, and unobserved by most of the sexually mature population, and consequently promote and encourage lawlessness. Ordinary common sense tells us there are not and never could be enough policemen, enough jails, enough judges or enough courts to take care of even a tiny segment of the 95 percent of sexually mature males alone who break one or more of the sex laws.

3. Sex education is imperative for most Americans. The public is appallingly ignorant of the sexual nature of man, having little knowledge of its biological and psychological significance in the living of a healthy and happy life. Ministers, priests, lawmakers, parents, and even teachers of sex in those public schools where the subject of sex is allowed to be taught are woefully lacking in knowledge or understanding of its vast significance. It is a well-known fact that the unknown and the mysterious create fear in the mind of man, that, in other words, fear thrives on ignorance. Natural fears are essential in man's struggle to survive and are in themselves a self-defense mechanism, but because man's sexual knowledge has been based on false beliefs, he has developed a host of unnatural and irrational sexual fears that can only be erased from his mind by the biological and psychological discoveries of recent years.

A uniform, national program of sex education of a practical, prudent, and realistic nature that conforms with the natural laws of human sexuality could be developed by a Committee of nationally known authorities and offered in all schools. Universities and colleges should offer courses and degrees on sexology and produce specially trained social workers and teachers for the public schools. Ministers and priests should be trained in sexology while still in the seminary in order that they may offer intelligent and realistic instruction on the spiritual aspects of sexuality based on biological and psychological facts. Doctors should be taught how important a natural sexual life is for both physical and mental health.

Once these avenues of sex education have been established, the unhealthy and unrealistic sex attitudes of the public could be erased, and a mentally and physically healthy and natural acceptance of sex could eventually be established, freeing us from the unnecessary misery caused by unnatural and irrational fears.

No earthquake, no famine, no calamity caused by nature could measure up to the unimaginable accumulation of suffering man causes himself because of false sexual beliefs and his deplorable lack of sexual knowledge. We have the knowledge, but, unfortunately, a large percentage of religious and legal authorities—those who have the power, authority, and influence to revitalize society by adopting, realistic sexual mores to harmonize with the natural laws of human sexuality—seemingly have sealed their minds against the changes warranted by recently discovered facts, or simply make no effort to acquaint themselves with the biology and psychology of sex.

Without knowledge of the role human sexuality plays in physical and mental health, it is not even possible to imagine the cumulative horrors of drug addiction, alcoholism, the sexual frustration and fears of teenagers, divorce and broken homes, the savagery and violence of sadism, the pitiful suicides, the mental torture of homosexuals, the inhumanity of vicious sexual gossip, the terrorizing effects on the population by crime and violence, and the other social disasters stemming from sexual fears and frustrations.

It is a pity that sexually ignorant religious and political figures lash out at the increasing immorality and corruption without the least idea of how to remedy the situation. They have no comprehension or realization of the fact that the more we try to suppress the sex urge the surer it is that the sex urge will control us. The laws of inversion automatically make this inevitable. The excesses we call sexual immorality are the results. In our ignorance we are actually inviting and forcing, in the form of sexual promiscuity and sexual exhibitionism, the very same sexual immorality so many of us are shocked and horrified at. What we call a sexual revolution is not a revolution but a rebellion against the unnatural suppression of the sex urge.

A true sexual revolution will include an entirely new and realistic code of sexual morals recognizing the fact that man was created by God to be a sexual being. It will include the recognition of sex as a natural function and a human instinct provided by God for human joy and happiness. It will include the complete revision of religious beliefs and criminal laws that are in conflict with modern biological and psychological facts and principles. It will include the abolition of the theory that sex activity is sinful and criminal even when it does not harm other human beings or does not disturb or affect the public welfare. It will eliminate all unnatural shame, unnatural sexual guilt, and irrational sexual fears. It will recognize the necessity for complete and sufficient release of sexual tensions as a requirement for good mental and physical health. It will recognize the sex drive as the source of all human love—a love that would balance and neutralize the aggressions of the self-preservation drive. It will recognize that human beings are biologically conditioned to be sexual beings with the sex drive at the core of their existence.

There is one vital fact that we must recognize—we will never replace the hate that fills the world with love if we keep fearing our God-given sexuality—the source of all human love.

St. John, in his first epistle, observes, "There is no fear in love; but perfect love casts out fear because fear brings on punishment. And he who fears is not perfected in love."

phlet). A frank discussion of various sex problems.

Duffy, Clinton T., with Al Hirshberg. *Sex and Crime.* Doubleday, 1965. A startling exposure of sex problems as the basic cause of most crime, written by a famous prison warden and penologist.

Eckert, Ralph G. *Sex Attitudes in the Home.* American Press, 1956. Practical answers for parents in guiding children toward developing positive attitudes to sex and love in the home.

Ellis, Albert. *The American Sexual Tragedy.* Twayne, 1954. An account of the distortions, frustrations and broken homes caused by sexual ignorance and false conceptions of sex.
Sex Without Guilt. Lyle Stuart, 1958. An account of condemned sexual practices that are neither harmful in themselves nor in others but that are the unnecessary cause of demoralizing anxieties and fears.

Fishman, Joseph F. *Sex in Prison.* National Library Press, 1934. An informative and often shocking exposure of the sexual starvation of prisoners, with its inevitable aftermath of homosexuality or inhuman suffering.

Freeman, Lucy. *Before I Kill More.* Crown Publishers, Inc., 1955. The remarkable account of Bill Heirens, the sensational Chicago boy murderer. It is a fascinating exploration of the buried fears and dark corners in the mind of a tortured soul and an outstanding example of a fantastic sexual perversion caused by a blocked sex drive—blocked by a strong religious conviction that all sex was evil.

Gebhard, Paul H. *Sex Offenders* (Kinsey Report). Harper & Row, 1965. The first truly objective, detailed and diversified study of sex offenders, based on personal interviews with over 1,500 convicted breakers of sex laws.

Goldberg, B. Z. *The Story of Sex in Religion.* Grove Press Inc., 1962. The author shows how sex and religion have been inseparably intertwined all through the history of mankind and how religion itself owes its origin and early development to sex. His thesis is that sex, properly controlled, not despised and condemned, would give new life to old and decadent religions.

Henley, Arthur. *Demon in My View.* Trident Press, 1966. An absorbing account of the rehabilitation of disturbed children, who had been pronounced incurable, by the magic powers of love, affection and understanding. The sexual aspects of some of the cases are fascinating.

Hunt, Morton M. "Castration: Man's Greatest Hidden Fear." *Man's Magazine,* November 1956. Unconscious fear of castration is deeply ingrained in every human male. The peak of vengeance in wars has been mutilation of the enemy's genitals.

Kinsey, Alfred. *Sexual Behavior in the Human Male.* W. B. Saunders Co., 1948. A study of the sexual behavior of the human male from a biological standpoint and scientist's viewpoint without moral bias or prejudice derived from society's present taboos.

Lawton, Shailer Upton. "A Psychiatrist Looks at Sex Humor." *Man's Magazine,* September 1958. A frank appraisal of one of man's most popular pastimes.

Lewinsohn, Richard. *A History of Sexual Customs.* Harper & Bros., 1958. Sex in all of its scope and detail is discussed and traced into all the fields bordering sex, such as the arts, the social structure, law, medicine, superstition and custom, and historical change.

Lindner, Robert M. *Rebel Without a Cause.* Grune & Stratton, 1944. The remarkable account of the hypnoanalysis of a criminal psychopath. It shows that criminality can have its roots in a shocking sexual incident at the age of nine months.

Malinowski, Bronislaw. *The Sexual Life of Savages in Northwestern Melanesia.* Eugenics Pub. Co., 1929. In this classic, Malinowski relates the results of his extensive investigation of the complete sexual life of the uncivilized Trobrianders in its aesthetic, emotional, family, and social implications. The natives, unaffected by being Christianized or following Christian sexual codes, had no sexual perversions, functional psychosis, or psychoneurosis, no sexual murders, no word for theft; masturbation and homosexuality were simply imperfect means of sexual release.

Maxey, Wallace de Ortega. *Man Is a Sexual Being.* Fabian Books, 1958. Man will inevitably seek outlets for sexual gratification in one way or another, because he is predominantly a sexual being.

McHugh, Gelolo, with Moskin, Robert J. "What Americans Need to Learn About Sex." *Collier's,* November 9, 1956. The report on a scientific study of American sexual knowledge; it found that even well-educated Americans are tangled in a web of taboos, superstitions and misinformation.

"What Ministers Are Learning About Sex." *Look,* November 25, 1958. A shocking report on the inadequate sexual knowledge of Protestant ministers.

Menninger, Karl. *Love Against Hate.* Harcourt Brace & Co., 1942. An analysis of the war of emotions within each of us and how the power of love can shape our instinctive aggressiveness to the service of human happiness.

Mines, Robert. "What Drives Men into Sex Panics?" *Real Magazine,* April 1954. Sex panics analyzed as explosive crises affecting one man in ten and leading to violence and crime—even murder and suicide. Although seldom discussed in print they are very real psychological occurrences that doctors encounter time and again.

Montagu, Ashley. *Touching—The Human Significance of the Skin.* Columbia University Press, 1971. A study of the importance of tactile sensations in human behavior.

Morse, Benjamin. *The Sexual Deviate.* Lancer Books, 1963. A nontechnical, easy-to-read book concerning the various types of sexual deviations and perversions and their nature.

Morris, Desmond. *The Naked Ape.* McGraw Hill Book Co., 1967. In chapter 2 the author describes the sexual behavior of humans before and during the sex act.

Moskin, J. Robert. "The Danes' Bold Experiment: Legalized Pornography." *Look,* July 29, 1969. A very illuminating article about Denmark's abandonment of all restrictions on pornography on the very realistic theory that prohibition stimulates interest in it and it is smarter to make it more legitimate and less tantalizing.

Payne, James E. "You Can't Run Away From Sex." *Popular Medicine,* April 1956. A brilliant article on the place of sex in the health and happiness of human beings, showing how it can be the most constructive force in the life of man—or the most destructive.

lummer, Douglas. *Queer People.* Citadel Press, 1965. A subjective approach to the feelings and life of a homosexual in plain language and without apology. It tells what it feels like to be a homosexual today and describes the type of life a homosexual must lead.

Priestly, J. B. "Eroticism, Sex and Love." *Saturday Evening Post,* April 27, 1963. Explanation of how the encouragement and exploitation of eroticism for commercial gain instead of natural healthy sex constitutes one of the worst features of Western civilization.

Putney, Snell and Gail. "Never Marry for Love." *Cosmopolitan,* June 1964. An explanation how love is one of man's most devastating inventions and marriage for love one of man's greatest pitfalls.

Radcliff, J. D. "This Makes the Man." *Argosy,* December 1950. A description of the two small glands that control the life and happiness of the male, the most remarkable of all body organs—the male testes.

Reich, Wilhelm. *The Function of the Orgasm.* Orgone Institute Press, 1948. A study of the orgasm and the affects of improper release of sexual tensions on the human body and on society as a whole.

Reynolds, Quentin. *Courtroom.* Garden City Books, 1950. The Greenfield Case (pp. 170-77) shows that the sex drive is active in a hopeless, epileptic imbecile without a brain.

Roeburt, John. *Sex Life and the Criminal Law.* Belmont Books. 1963. The author explains that the United States penal laws show little understanding or rational capacity for dealing with the various types of so-called sex crimes.

Souls, James R., Jr. "The Crime of Feeling Guilty." *Realife Guide,* February 1960. The case history of a homosexual, showing the terrible affects of guilt and fear caused by society's intolerance.

Urban, Rudolph von. "The Problem of Masturbation." *Realife Guide,* July 1958. A realistic discussion of this universal practice, explaining why it is necessary for the relief of sexual tensions caused by full sex glands, especially in children.

West, Donald J. *The Other Man.* Whiteside, Inc., 1955. A nontechnical, unbiased study of the social, legal and clinical aspects of homosexuality in the light of modern scientific knowledge.

Watson, John. "Can You Have Too Much Sex? *Realife Guide.* It is pointed out that the frequency of sexual intercourse is a matter of individual capacity.

Wexler, Susan Stanhope. *The Story of Sandy.* Signet Books, 1957. One of the most remarkable true stories ever told. It is both an appalling story of parental rejection of a child and a dramatic demonstration of the power of love. It also proves that parents can make or break their children in their first few years of life.

Woodward, L. T. *Ninety Percent of What You Know About Sex Is Wrong.* Parliament Books Inc., 1962. Myths, fancies and superstitions are destroyed in this frank book concerning man's most intimate questions on sex and marital love.

Wolfenden Report of the Committee on Homosexual Offenses and Prostitution. Lancer Books, 1964. A British survey of homosexuality carried out through the pressure of the Church of England's Moral Welfare Council, for the British Parliament. It is recommended that homosexuality between consenting adults be made a legal form of sexuality.